C-4708   CAREER EXAMINATION SERIES

This is your
PASSBOOK for...

Emergency Services Dispatcher

Test Preparation Study Guide
Questions & Answers

NLC®

NATIONAL LEARNING CORPORATION®

COPYRIGHT NOTICE

This book is SOLELY intended for, is sold ONLY to, and its use is RESTRICTED to individual, bona fide applicants or candidates who qualify by virtue of having seriously filed applications for appropriate license, certificate, professional and/or promotional advancement, higher school matriculation, scholarship, or other legitimate requirements of education and/or governmental authorities.

This book is NOT intended for use, class instruction, tutoring, training, duplication, copying, reprinting, excerption, or adaptation, etc., by:

1) Other publishers
2) Proprietors and/or Instructors of "Coaching" and/or Preparatory Courses
3) Personnel and/or Training Divisions of commercial, industrial, and governmental organizations
4) Schools, colleges, or universities and/or their departments and staffs, including teachers and other personnel
5) Testing Agencies or Bureaus
6) Study groups which seek by the purchase of a single volume to copy and/or duplicate and/or adapt this material for use by the group as a whole without having purchased individual volumes for each of the members of the group
7) Et al.

Such persons would be in violation of appropriate Federal and State statutes.

PROVISION OF LICENSING AGREEMENTS – Recognized educational, commercial, industrial, and governmental institutions and organizations, and others legitimately engaged in educational pursuits, including training, testing, and measurement activities, may address request for a licensing agreement to the copyright owners, who will determine whether, and under what conditions, including fees and charges, the materials in this book may be used them. In other words, a licensing facility exists for the legitimate use of the material in this book on other than an individual basis. However, it is asseverated and affirmed here that the material in this book CANNOT be used without the receipt of the express permission of such a licensing agreement from the Publishers. Inquiries re licensing should be addressed to the company, attention rights and permissions department.

All rights reserved, including the right of reproduction in whole or in part, in any form or by any means, electronic or mechanical, including photocopying, recording, or by any information storage and retrieval system, without permission in writing from the Publisher.

Copyright © 2023 by
National Learning Corporation

212 Michael Drive, Syosset, NY 11791
(516) 921-8888 • www.passbooks.com
E-mail: info@passbooks.com

PUBLISHED IN THE UNITED STATES OF AMERICA

PASSBOOK® SERIES

THE *PASSBOOK® SERIES* has been created to prepare applicants and candidates for the ultimate academic battlefield – the examination room.

At some time in our lives, each and every one of us may be required to take an examination – for validation, matriculation, admission, qualification, registration, certification, or licensure.

Based on the assumption that every applicant or candidate has met the basic formal educational standards, has taken the required number of courses, and read the necessary texts, the *PASSBOOK® SERIES* furnishes the one special preparation which may assure passing with confidence, instead of failing with insecurity. Examination questions – together with answers – are furnished as the basic vehicle for study so that the mysteries of the examination and its compounding difficulties may be eliminated or diminished by a sure method.

This book is meant to help you pass your examination provided that you qualify and are serious in your objective.

The entire field is reviewed through the huge store of content information which is succinctly presented through a provocative and challenging approach – the question-and-answer method.

A climate of success is established by furnishing the correct answers at the end of each test.

You soon learn to recognize types of questions, forms of questions, and patterns of questioning. You may even begin to anticipate expected outcomes.

You perceive that many questions are repeated or adapted so that you can gain acute insights, which may enable you to score many sure points.

You learn how to confront new questions, or types of questions, and to attack them confidently and work out the correct answers.

You note objectives and emphases, and recognize pitfalls and dangers, so that you may make positive educational adjustments.

Moreover, you are kept fully informed in relation to new concepts, methods, practices, and directions in the field.

You discover that you are actually taking the examination all the time: you are preparing for the examination by "taking" an examination, not by reading extraneous and/or supererogatory textbooks.

In short, this PASSBOOK®, used directedly, should be an important factor in helping you to pass your test.

EMERGENCY SERVICES DISPATCHER

DUTIES:
This is highly responsible and periodically stressful work requiring the use of various types of telephonic, radio, and automatic signaling and communications equipment to receive and record emergency calls for assistance, and to dispatch appropriate personnel and equipment to emergencies. The incumbent must be computer literate, able to multi-task, and be readily able to learn to operate telephonic, radio, and automatic signaling communications devices in accordance with established procedures. The incumbent must be able to function calmly in emergencies and take appropriate action in an effective manner. The work is performed on a rotating shift basis which may include shifts on holidays and weekends as well as the evening and midnight hours, and may be required to work alternate shifts through and/or during off duty hours in the event of a major disaster. General supervision is received from the Senior Emergency Communications Dispatcher and/or the Emergency Services Director. The incumbent does related work as required.

SUBJECTS OF EXAMINATION:
The written test is designed to evaluate knowledge, skills and /or abilities in the following areas:
1. **Coding/decoding information** - These questions test for the ability to follow a set of coding rules. Some questions will require you to code information by converting certain information into letters or numbers. Other questions will require you to decode information by determining if the information that has already been converted into letters or numbers is correct. Complete directions will be provided; no previous knowledge of or training in any coding system is required.
2. **Following directions (maps)** - These questions test your ability to follow physical/geographic directions using street maps or building maps. You will have to read and understand a set of directions and then use them on a simple map.
3. **Retaining and comprehending spoken information from calls for emergency services** - These questions test for your ability to retain specific information that is heard in calls for emergency service, such as a street address, or to comprehend spoken information from emergency service calls, such as determining the location of a site in relation to landmarks. Simulated 911 calls will be played on audio CD. Immediately following each call, candidates are given audio instructions identifying which questions they are to answer within the test booklet. The questions that candidates are directed to answer for each simulated call will not be in sequential order. Candidates will need to retain and comprehend the information and instruction provided in this portion of the test to respond appropriately to the questions asked and to determine which questions to answer. The time allotted to answer these questions will be limited. At the end of each answer period, the CD will automatically play the next call. Note paper will be provided. Candidates will be permitted to take notes and to refer to them when answering the questions.
4. **Name and number checking** - These questions test for the ability to distinguish between sets of words, letters, and/or numbers that are almost exactly alike. Material is usually presented in two or three columns, and you will have to determine how the entry in the first column compares with the entry in the second column and possibly the third. You will be instructed to mark your answers according to a designated code provided in the directions.

HOW TO TAKE A TEST

I. YOU MUST PASS AN EXAMINATION

A. *WHAT EVERY CANDIDATE SHOULD KNOW*

Examination applicants often ask us for help in preparing for the written test. What can I study in advance? What kinds of questions will be asked? How will the test be given? How will the papers be graded?

As an applicant for a civil service examination, you may be wondering about some of these things. Our purpose here is to suggest effective methods of advance study and to describe civil service examinations.

Your chances for success on this examination can be increased if you know how to prepare. Those "pre-examination jitters" can be reduced if you know what to expect. You can even experience an adventure in good citizenship if you know why civil service exams are given.

B. *WHY ARE CIVIL SERVICE EXAMINATIONS GIVEN?*

Civil service examinations are important to you in two ways. As a citizen, you want public jobs filled by employees who know how to do their work. As a job seeker, you want a fair chance to compete for that job on an equal footing with other candidates. The best-known means of accomplishing this two-fold goal is the competitive examination.

Exams are widely publicized throughout the nation. They may be administered for jobs in federal, state, city, municipal, town or village governments or agencies.

Any citizen may apply, with some limitations, such as the age or residence of applicants. Your experience and education may be reviewed to see whether you meet the requirements for the particular examination. When these requirements exist, they are reasonable and applied consistently to all applicants. Thus, a competitive examination may cause you some uneasiness now, but it is your privilege and safeguard.

C. *HOW ARE CIVIL SERVICE EXAMS DEVELOPED?*

Examinations are carefully written by trained technicians who are specialists in the field known as "psychological measurement," in consultation with recognized authorities in the field of work that the test will cover. These experts recommend the subject matter areas or skills to be tested; only those knowledges or skills important to your success on the job are included. The most reliable books and source materials available are used as references. Together, the experts and technicians judge the difficulty level of the questions.

Test technicians know how to phrase questions so that the problem is clearly stated. Their ethics do not permit "trick" or "catch" questions. Questions may have been tried out on sample groups, or subjected to statistical analysis, to determine their usefulness.

Written tests are often used in combination with performance tests, ratings of training and experience, and oral interviews. All of these measures combine to form the best-known means of finding the right person for the right job.

II. HOW TO PASS THE WRITTEN TEST

A. NATURE OF THE EXAMINATION

To prepare intelligently for civil service examinations, you should know how they differ from school examinations you have taken. In school you were assigned certain definite pages to read or subjects to cover. The examination questions were quite detailed and usually emphasized memory. Civil service exams, on the other hand, try to discover your present ability to perform the duties of a position, plus your potentiality to learn these duties. In other words, a civil service exam attempts to predict how successful you will be. Questions cover such a broad area that they cannot be as minute and detailed as school exam questions.

In the public service similar kinds of work, or positions, are grouped together in one "class." This process is known as *position-classification*. All the positions in a class are paid according to the salary range for that class. One class title covers all of these positions, and they are all tested by the same examination.

B. FOUR BASIC STEPS

1) Study the announcement

How, then, can you know what subjects to study? Our best answer is: "Learn as much as possible about the class of positions for which you've applied." The exam will test the knowledge, skills and abilities needed to do the work.

Your most valuable source of information about the position you want is the official exam announcement. This announcement lists the training and experience qualifications. Check these standards and apply only if you come reasonably close to meeting them.

The brief description of the position in the examination announcement offers some clues to the subjects which will be tested. Think about the job itself. Review the duties in your mind. Can you perform them, or are there some in which you are rusty? Fill in the blank spots in your preparation.

Many jurisdictions preview the written test in the exam announcement by including a section called "Knowledge and Abilities Required," "Scope of the Examination," or some similar heading. Here you will find out specifically what fields will be tested.

2) Review your own background

Once you learn in general what the position is all about, and what you need to know to do the work, ask yourself which subjects you already know fairly well and which need improvement. You may wonder whether to concentrate on improving your strong areas or on building some background in your fields of weakness. When the announcement has specified "some knowledge" or "considerable knowledge," or has used adjectives like "beginning principles of..." or "advanced ... methods," you can get a clue as to the number and difficulty of questions to be asked in any given field. More questions, and hence broader coverage, would be included for those subjects which are more important in the work. Now weigh your strengths and weaknesses against the job requirements and prepare accordingly.

3) Determine the level of the position

Another way to tell how intensively you should prepare is to understand the level of the job for which you are applying. Is it the entering level? In other words, is this the position in which beginners in a field of work are hired? Or is it an intermediate or advanced level? Sometimes this is indicated by such words as "Junior" or "Senior" in the class title. Other jurisdictions use Roman numerals to designate the level – Clerk I, Clerk II, for example. The word "Supervisor" sometimes appears in the title. If the level is not indicated by the title, check the description of duties. Will you be working under very close supervision, or will you have responsibility for independent decisions in this work?

4) Choose appropriate study materials

Now that you know the subjects to be examined and the relative amount of each subject to be covered, you can choose suitable study materials. For beginning level jobs, or even advanced ones, if you have a pronounced weakness in some aspect of your training, read a modern, standard textbook in that field. Be sure it is up to date and has general coverage. Such books are normally available at your library, and the librarian will be glad to help you locate one. For entry-level positions, questions of appropriate difficulty are chosen – neither highly advanced questions, nor those too simple. Such questions require careful thought but not advanced training.

If the position for which you are applying is technical or advanced, you will read more advanced, specialized material. If you are already familiar with the basic principles of your field, elementary textbooks would waste your time. Concentrate on advanced textbooks and technical periodicals. Think through the concepts and review difficult problems in your field.

These are all general sources. You can get more ideas on your own initiative, following these leads. For example, training manuals and publications of the government agency which employs workers in your field can be useful, particularly for technical and professional positions. A letter or visit to the government department involved may result in more specific study suggestions, and certainly will provide you with a more definite idea of the exact nature of the position you are seeking.

III. KINDS OF TESTS

Tests are used for purposes other than measuring knowledge and ability to perform specified duties. For some positions, it is equally important to test ability to make adjustments to new situations or to profit from training. In others, basic mental abilities not dependent on information are essential. Questions which test these things may not appear as pertinent to the duties of the position as those which test for knowledge and information. Yet they are often highly important parts of a fair examination. For very general questions, it is almost impossible to help you direct your study efforts. What we can do is to point out some of the more common of these general abilities needed in public service positions and describe some typical questions.

1) General information

Broad, general information has been found useful for predicting job success in some kinds of work. This is tested in a variety of ways, from vocabulary lists to questions about current events. Basic background in some field of work, such as sociology or economics, may be sampled in a group of questions. Often these are principles which have become familiar to most persons through exposure rather than through formal training. It is difficult to advise you how to study for these questions; being alert to the world around you is our best suggestion.

2) Verbal ability

An example of an ability needed in many positions is verbal or language ability. Verbal ability is, in brief, the ability to use and understand words. Vocabulary and grammar tests are typical measures of this ability. Reading comprehension or paragraph interpretation questions are common in many kinds of civil service tests. You are given a paragraph of written material and asked to find its central meaning.

3) Numerical ability
Number skills can be tested by the familiar arithmetic problem, by checking paired lists of numbers to see which are alike and which are different, or by interpreting charts and graphs. In the latter test, a graph may be printed in the test booklet which you are asked to use as the basis for answering questions.

4) Observation
A popular test for law-enforcement positions is the observation test. A picture is shown to you for several minutes, then taken away. Questions about the picture test your ability to observe both details and larger elements.

5) Following directions
In many positions in the public service, the employee must be able to carry out written instructions dependably and accurately. You may be given a chart with several columns, each column listing a variety of information. The questions require you to carry out directions involving the information given in the chart.

6) Skills and aptitudes
Performance tests effectively measure some manual skills and aptitudes. When the skill is one in which you are trained, such as typing or shorthand, you can practice. These tests are often very much like those given in business school or high school courses. For many of the other skills and aptitudes, however, no short-time preparation can be made. Skills and abilities natural to you or that you have developed throughout your lifetime are being tested.

Many of the general questions just described provide all the data needed to answer the questions and ask you to use your reasoning ability to find the answers. Your best preparation for these tests, as well as for tests of facts and ideas, is to be at your physical and mental best. You, no doubt, have your own methods of getting into an exam-taking mood and keeping "in shape." The next section lists some ideas on this subject.

IV. KINDS OF QUESTIONS

Only rarely is the "essay" question, which you answer in narrative form, used in civil service tests. Civil service tests are usually of the short-answer type. Full instructions for answering these questions will be given to you at the examination. But in case this is your first experience with short-answer questions and separate answer sheets, here is what you need to know:

1) Multiple-choice Questions
Most popular of the short-answer questions is the "multiple choice" or "best answer" question. It can be used, for example, to test for factual knowledge, ability to solve problems or judgment in meeting situations found at work.

A multiple-choice question is normally one of three types—
- It can begin with an incomplete statement followed by several possible endings. You are to find the one ending which *best* completes the statement, although some of the others may not be entirely wrong.
- It can also be a complete statement in the form of a question which is answered by choosing one of the statements listed.

- It can be in the form of a problem – again you select the best answer.

Here is an example of a multiple-choice question with a discussion which should give you some clues as to the method for choosing the right answer:

When an employee has a complaint about his assignment, the action which will *best* help him overcome his difficulty is to
- A. discuss his difficulty with his coworkers
- B. take the problem to the head of the organization
- C. take the problem to the person who gave him the assignment
- D. say nothing to anyone about his complaint

In answering this question, you should study each of the choices to find which is best. Consider choice "A" – Certainly an employee may discuss his complaint with fellow employees, but no change or improvement can result, and the complaint remains unresolved. Choice "B" is a poor choice since the head of the organization probably does not know what assignment you have been given, and taking your problem to him is known as "going over the head" of the supervisor. The supervisor, or person who made the assignment, is the person who can clarify it or correct any injustice. Choice "C" is, therefore, correct. To say nothing, as in choice "D," is unwise. Supervisors have and interest in knowing the problems employees are facing, and the employee is seeking a solution to his problem.

2) True/False Questions

The "true/false" or "right/wrong" form of question is sometimes used. Here a complete statement is given. Your job is to decide whether the statement is right or wrong.

SAMPLE: A roaming cell-phone call to a nearby city costs less than a non-roaming call to a distant city.

This statement is wrong, or false, since roaming calls are more expensive.

This is not a complete list of all possible question forms, although most of the others are variations of these common types. You will always get complete directions for answering questions. Be sure you understand *how* to mark your answers – ask questions until you do.

V. RECORDING YOUR ANSWERS

Computer terminals are used more and more today for many different kinds of exams.

For an examination with very few applicants, you may be told to record your answers in the test booklet itself. Separate answer sheets are much more common. If this separate answer sheet is to be scored by machine – and this is often the case – it is highly important that you mark your answers correctly in order to get credit.

An electronic scoring machine is often used in civil service offices because of the speed with which papers can be scored. Machine-scored answer sheets must be marked with a pencil, which will be given to you. This pencil has a high graphite content which responds to the electronic scoring machine. As a matter of fact, stray dots may register as answers, so do not let your pencil rest on the answer sheet while you are pondering the correct answer. Also, if your pencil lead breaks or is otherwise defective, ask for another.

Since the answer sheet will be dropped in a slot in the scoring machine, be careful not to bend the corners or get the paper crumpled.

The answer sheet normally has five vertical columns of numbers, with 30 numbers to a column. These numbers correspond to the question numbers in your test booklet. After each number, going across the page are four or five pairs of dotted lines. These short dotted lines have small letters or numbers above them. The first two pairs may also have a "T" or "F" above the letters. This indicates that the first two pairs only are to be used if the questions are of the true-false type. If the questions are multiple choice, disregard the "T" and "F" and pay attention only to the small letters or numbers.

Answer your questions in the manner of the sample that follows:

32. The largest city in the United States is
    A. Washington, D.C.
    B. New York City
    C. Chicago
    D. Detroit
    E. San Francisco

1) Choose the answer you think is best. (New York City is the largest, so "B" is correct.)
2) Find the row of dotted lines numbered the same as the question you are answering. (Find row number 32)
3) Find the pair of dotted lines corresponding to the answer. (Find the pair of lines under the mark "B.")
4) Make a solid black mark between the dotted lines.

VI. BEFORE THE TEST

Common sense will help you find procedures to follow to get ready for an examination. Too many of us, however, overlook these sensible measures. Indeed, nervousness and fatigue have been found to be the most serious reasons why applicants fail to do their best on civil service tests. Here is a list of reminders:

- Begin your preparation early – Don't wait until the last minute to go scurrying around for books and materials or to find out what the position is all about.
- Prepare continuously – An hour a night for a week is better than an all-night cram session. This has been definitely established. What is more, a night a week for a month will return better dividends than crowding your study into a shorter period of time.
- Locate the place of the exam – You have been sent a notice telling you when and where to report for the examination. If the location is in a different town or otherwise unfamiliar to you, it would be well to inquire the best route and learn something about the building.
- Relax the night before the test – Allow your mind to rest. Do not study at all that night. Plan some mild recreation or diversion; then go to bed early and get a good night's sleep.
- Get up early enough to make a leisurely trip to the place for the test – This way unforeseen events, traffic snarls, unfamiliar buildings, etc. will not upset you.
- Dress comfortably – A written test is not a fashion show. You will be known by number and not by name, so wear something comfortable.

- Leave excess paraphernalia at home – Shopping bags and odd bundles will get in your way. You need bring only the items mentioned in the official notice you received; usually everything you need is provided. Do not bring reference books to the exam. They will only confuse those last minutes and be taken away from you when in the test room.
- Arrive somewhat ahead of time – If because of transportation schedules you must get there very early, bring a newspaper or magazine to take your mind off yourself while waiting.
- Locate the examination room – When you have found the proper room, you will be directed to the seat or part of the room where you will sit. Sometimes you are given a sheet of instructions to read while you are waiting. Do not fill out any forms until you are told to do so; just read them and be prepared.
- Relax and prepare to listen to the instructions
- If you have any physical problem that may keep you from doing your best, be sure to tell the test administrator. If you are sick or in poor health, you really cannot do your best on the exam. You can come back and take the test some other time.

VII. AT THE TEST

The day of the test is here and you have the test booklet in your hand. The temptation to get going is very strong. Caution! There is more to success than knowing the right answers. You must know how to identify your papers and understand variations in the type of short-answer question used in this particular examination. Follow these suggestions for maximum results from your efforts:

1) Cooperate with the monitor

The test administrator has a duty to create a situation in which you can be as much at ease as possible. He will give instructions, tell you when to begin, check to see that you are marking your answer sheet correctly, and so on. He is not there to guard you, although he will see that your competitors do not take unfair advantage. He wants to help you do your best.

2) Listen to all instructions

Don't jump the gun! Wait until you understand all directions. In most civil service tests you get more time than you need to answer the questions. So don't be in a hurry. Read each word of instructions until you clearly understand the meaning. Study the examples, listen to all announcements and follow directions. Ask questions if you do not understand what to do.

3) Identify your papers

Civil service exams are usually identified by number only. You will be assigned a number; you must not put your name on your test papers. Be sure to copy your number correctly. Since more than one exam may be given, copy your exact examination title.

4) Plan your time

Unless you are told that a test is a "speed" or "rate of work" test, speed itself is usually not important. Time enough to answer all the questions will be provided, but this does not mean that you have all day. An overall time limit has been set. Divide the total time (in minutes) by the number of questions to determine the approximate time you have for each question.

5) Do not linger over difficult questions

If you come across a difficult question, mark it with a paper clip (useful to have along) and come back to it when you have been through the booklet. One caution if you do this – be sure to skip a number on your answer sheet as well. Check often to be sure that you have not lost your place and that you are marking in the row numbered the same as the question you are answering.

6) Read the questions

Be sure you know what the question asks! Many capable people are unsuccessful because they failed to *read* the questions correctly.

7) Answer all questions

Unless you have been instructed that a penalty will be deducted for incorrect answers, it is better to guess than to omit a question.

8) Speed tests

It is often better NOT to guess on speed tests. It has been found that on timed tests people are tempted to spend the last few seconds before time is called in marking answers at random – without even reading them – in the hope of picking up a few extra points. To discourage this practice, the instructions may warn you that your score will be "corrected" for guessing. That is, a penalty will be applied. The incorrect answers will be deducted from the correct ones, or some other penalty formula will be used.

9) Review your answers

If you finish before time is called, go back to the questions you guessed or omitted to give them further thought. Review other answers if you have time.

10) Return your test materials

If you are ready to leave before others have finished or time is called, take ALL your materials to the monitor and leave quietly. Never take any test material with you. The monitor can discover whose papers are not complete, and taking a test booklet may be grounds for disqualification.

VIII. EXAMINATION TECHNIQUES

1) Read the general instructions carefully. These are usually printed on the first page of the exam booklet. As a rule, these instructions refer to the timing of the examination; the fact that you should not start work until the signal and must stop work at a signal, etc. If there are any *special* instructions, such as a choice of questions to be answered, make sure that you note this instruction carefully.

2) When you are ready to start work on the examination, that is as soon as the signal has been given, read the instructions to each question booklet, underline any key words or phrases, such as *least, best, outline, describe* and the like. In this way you will tend to answer as requested rather than discover on reviewing your paper that you *listed without describing*, that you selected the *worst* choice rather than the *best* choice, etc.

3) If the examination is of the objective or multiple-choice type – that is, each question will also give a series of possible answers: A, B, C or D, and you are called upon to select the best answer and write the letter next to that answer on your answer paper – it is advisable to start answering each question in turn. There may be anywhere from 50 to 100 such questions in the three or four hours allotted and you can see how much time would be taken if you read through all the questions before beginning to answer any. Furthermore, if you come across a question or group of questions which you know would be difficult to answer, it would undoubtedly affect your handling of all the other questions.

4) If the examination is of the essay type and contains but a few questions, it is a moot point as to whether you should read all the questions before starting to answer any one. Of course, if you are given a choice – say five out of seven and the like – then it is essential to read all the questions so you can eliminate the two that are most difficult. If, however, you are asked to answer all the questions, there may be danger in trying to answer the easiest one first because you may find that you will spend too much time on it. The best technique is to answer the first question, then proceed to the second, etc.

5) Time your answers. Before the exam begins, write down the time it started, then add the time allowed for the examination and write down the time it must be completed, then divide the time available somewhat as follows:
    - If 3-1/2 hours are allowed, that would be 210 minutes. If you have 80 objective-type questions, that would be an average of 2-1/2 minutes per question. Allow yourself no more than 2 minutes per question, or a total of 160 minutes, which will permit about 50 minutes to review.
    - If for the time allotment of 210 minutes there are 7 essay questions to answer, that would average about 30 minutes a question. Give yourself only 25 minutes per question so that you have about 35 minutes to review.

6) The most important instruction is to *read each question* and make sure you know what is wanted. The second most important instruction is to *time yourself properly* so that you answer every question. The third most important instruction is to *answer every question*. Guess if you have to but include something for each question. Remember that you will receive no credit for a blank and will probably receive some credit if you write something in answer to an essay question. If you guess a letter – say "B" for a multiple-choice question – you may have guessed right. If you leave a blank as an answer to a multiple-choice question, the examiners may respect your feelings but it will not add a point to your score. Some exams may penalize you for wrong answers, so in such cases *only*, you may not want to guess unless you have some basis for your answer.

7) Suggestions
   a. Objective-type questions
      1. Examine the question booklet for proper sequence of pages and questions
      2. Read all instructions carefully
      3. Skip any question which seems too difficult; return to it after all other questions have been answered
      4. Apportion your time properly; do not spend too much time on any single question or group of questions

5. Note and underline key words – *all, most, fewest, least, best, worst, same, opposite,* etc.
6. Pay particular attention to negatives
7. Note unusual option, e.g., unduly long, short, complex, different or similar in content to the body of the question
8. Observe the use of "hedging" words – *probably, may, most likely,* etc.
9. Make sure that your answer is put next to the same number as the question
10. Do not second-guess unless you have good reason to believe the second answer is definitely more correct
11. Cross out original answer if you decide another answer is more accurate; do not erase until you are ready to hand your paper in
12. Answer all questions; guess unless instructed otherwise
13. Leave time for review

  b. Essay questions
    1. Read each question carefully
    2. Determine exactly what is wanted. Underline key words or phrases.
    3. Decide on outline or paragraph answer
    4. Include many different points and elements unless asked to develop any one or two points or elements
    5. Show impartiality by giving pros and cons unless directed to select one side only
    6. Make and write down any assumptions you find necessary to answer the questions
    7. Watch your English, grammar, punctuation and choice of words
    8. Time your answers; don't crowd material

8) Answering the essay question

Most essay questions can be answered by framing the specific response around several key words or ideas. Here are a few such key words or ideas:

M's: manpower, materials, methods, money, management
P's: purpose, program, policy, plan, procedure, practice, problems, pitfalls, personnel, public relations

  a. Six basic steps in handling problems:
    1. Preliminary plan and background development
    2. Collect information, data and facts
    3. Analyze and interpret information, data and facts
    4. Analyze and develop solutions as well as make recommendations
    5. Prepare report and sell recommendations
    6. Install recommendations and follow up effectiveness

  b. Pitfalls to avoid
    1. *Taking things for granted* – A statement of the situation does not necessarily imply that each of the elements is necessarily true; for example, a complaint may be invalid and biased so that all that can be taken for granted is that a complaint has been registered

2. *Considering only one side of a situation* – Wherever possible, indicate several alternatives and then point out the reasons you selected the best one
3. *Failing to indicate follow up* – Whenever your answer indicates action on your part, make certain that you will take proper follow-up action to see how successful your recommendations, procedures or actions turn out to be
4. *Taking too long in answering any single question* – Remember to time your answers properly

IX. AFTER THE TEST

Scoring procedures differ in detail among civil service jurisdictions although the general principles are the same. Whether the papers are hand-scored or graded by machine we have described, they are nearly always graded by number. That is, the person who marks the paper knows only the number – never the name – of the applicant. Not until all the papers have been graded will they be matched with names. If other tests, such as training and experience or oral interview ratings have been given, scores will be combined. Different parts of the examination usually have different weights. For example, the written test might count 60 percent of the final grade, and a rating of training and experience 40 percent. In many jurisdictions, veterans will have a certain number of points added to their grades.

After the final grade has been determined, the names are placed in grade order and an eligible list is established. There are various methods for resolving ties between those who get the same final grade – probably the most common is to place first the name of the person whose application was received first. Job offers are made from the eligible list in the order the names appear on it. You will be notified of your grade and your rank as soon as all these computations have been made. This will be done as rapidly as possible.

People who are found to meet the requirements in the announcement are called "eligibles." Their names are put on a list of eligible candidates. An eligible's chances of getting a job depend on how high he stands on this list and how fast agencies are filling jobs from the list.

When a job is to be filled from a list of eligibles, the agency asks for the names of people on the list of eligibles for that job. When the civil service commission receives this request, it sends to the agency the names of the three people highest on this list. Or, if the job to be filled has specialized requirements, the office sends the agency the names of the top three persons who meet these requirements from the general list.

The appointing officer makes a choice from among the three people whose names were sent to him. If the selected person accepts the appointment, the names of the others are put back on the list to be considered for future openings.

That is the rule in hiring from all kinds of eligible lists, whether they are for typist, carpenter, chemist, or something else. For every vacancy, the appointing officer has his choice of any one of the top three eligibles on the list. This explains why the person whose name is on top of the list sometimes does not get an appointment when some of the persons lower on the list do. If the appointing officer chooses the second or third eligible, the No. 1 eligible does not get a job at once, but stays on the list until he is appointed or the list is terminated.

X. HOW TO PASS THE INTERVIEW TEST

The examination for which you applied requires an oral interview test. You have already taken the written test and you are now being called for the interview test – the final part of the formal examination.

You may think that it is not possible to prepare for an interview test and that there are no procedures to follow during an interview. Our purpose is to point out some things you can do in advance that will help you and some good rules to follow and pitfalls to avoid while you are being interviewed.

What is an interview supposed to test?

The written examination is designed to test the technical knowledge and competence of the candidate; the oral is designed to evaluate intangible qualities, not readily measured otherwise, and to establish a list showing the relative fitness of each candidate – as measured against his competitors – for the position sought. Scoring is not on the basis of "right" and "wrong," but on a sliding scale of values ranging from "not passable" to "outstanding." As a matter of fact, it is possible to achieve a relatively low score without a single "incorrect" answer because of evident weakness in the qualities being measured.

Occasionally, an examination may consist entirely of an oral test – either an individual or a group oral. In such cases, information is sought concerning the technical knowledges and abilities of the candidate, since there has been no written examination for this purpose. More commonly, however, an oral test is used to supplement a written examination.

Who conducts interviews?

The composition of oral boards varies among different jurisdictions. In nearly all, a representative of the personnel department serves as chairman. One of the members of the board may be a representative of the department in which the candidate would work. In some cases, "outside experts" are used, and, frequently, a businessman or some other representative of the general public is asked to serve. Labor and management or other special groups may be represented. The aim is to secure the services of experts in the appropriate field.

However the board is composed, it is a good idea (and not at all improper or unethical) to ascertain in advance of the interview who the members are and what groups they represent. When you are introduced to them, you will have some idea of their backgrounds and interests, and at least you will not stutter and stammer over their names.

What should be done before the interview?

While knowledge about the board members is useful and takes some of the surprise element out of the interview, there is other preparation which is more substantive. It *is* possible to prepare for an oral interview – in several ways:

1) Keep a copy of your application and review it carefully before the interview

This may be the only document before the oral board, and the starting point of the interview. Know what education and experience you have listed there, and the sequence and dates of all of it. Sometimes the board will ask you to review the highlights of your experience for them; you should not have to hem and haw doing it.

2) Study the class specification and the examination announcement

Usually, the oral board has one or both of these to guide them. The qualities, characteristics or knowledges required by the position sought are stated in these documents. They offer valuable clues as to the nature of the oral interview. For example, if the job involves supervisory responsibilities, the announcement will usually indicate that knowledge of modern supervisory methods and the qualifications of the candidate as a supervisor will be tested. If so, you can expect such questions, frequently in the form of a hypothetical situation which you are expected to solve. NEVER go into an oral without knowledge of the duties and responsibilities of the job you seek.

3) Think through each qualification required

Try to visualize the kind of questions you would ask if you were a board member. How well could you answer them? Try especially to appraise your own knowledge and background in each area, *measured against the job sought*, and identify any areas in which you are weak. Be critical and realistic – do not flatter yourself.

4) Do some general reading in areas in which you feel you may be weak

For example, if the job involves supervision and your past experience has NOT, some general reading in supervisory methods and practices, particularly in the field of human relations, might be useful. Do NOT study agency procedures or detailed manuals. The oral board will be testing your understanding and capacity, not your memory.

5) Get a good night's sleep and watch your general health and mental attitude

You will want a clear head at the interview. Take care of a cold or any other minor ailment, and of course, no hangovers.

What should be done on the day of the interview?

Now comes the day of the interview itself. Give yourself plenty of time to get there. Plan to arrive somewhat ahead of the scheduled time, particularly if your appointment is in the fore part of the day. If a previous candidate fails to appear, the board might be ready for you a bit early. By early afternoon an oral board is almost invariably behind schedule if there are many candidates, and you may have to wait. Take along a book or magazine to read, or your application to review, but leave any extraneous material in the waiting room when you go in for your interview. In any event, relax and compose yourself.

The matter of dress is important. The board is forming impressions about you – from your experience, your manners, your attitude, and your appearance. Give your personal appearance careful attention. Dress your best, but not your flashiest. Choose conservative, appropriate clothing, and be sure it is immaculate. This is a business interview, and your appearance should indicate that you regard it as such. Besides, being well groomed and properly dressed will help boost your confidence.

Sooner or later, someone will call your name and escort you into the interview room. *This is it.* From here on you are on your own. It is too late for any more preparation. But remember, you asked for this opportunity to prove your fitness, and you are here because your request was granted.

What happens when you go in?

The usual sequence of events will be as follows: The clerk (who is often the board stenographer) will introduce you to the chairman of the oral board, who will introduce you to the other members of the board. Acknowledge the introductions before you sit down. Do not be surprised if you find a microphone facing you or a stenotypist sitting by. Oral interviews are usually recorded in the event of an appeal or other review.

Usually the chairman of the board will open the interview by reviewing the highlights of your education and work experience from your application – primarily for the benefit of the other members of the board, as well as to get the material into the record. Do not interrupt or comment unless there is an error or significant misinterpretation; if that is the case, do not hesitate. But do not quibble about insignificant matters. Also, he will usually ask you some question about your education, experience or your present job – partly to get you to start talking and to establish the interviewing "rapport." He may start the actual questioning, or turn it over to one of the other members. Frequently, each member undertakes the questioning on a particular area, one in which he is perhaps most competent, so you can expect each member to participate in the examination. Because time is limited, you may also expect some rather abrupt switches in the direction the questioning takes, so do not be upset by it. Normally, a board member will not pursue a single line of questioning unless he discovers a particular strength or weakness.

After each member has participated, the chairman will usually ask whether any member has any further questions, then will ask you if you have anything you wish to add. Unless you are expecting this question, it may floor you. Worse, it may start you off on an extended, extemporaneous speech. The board is not usually seeking more information. The question is principally to offer you a last opportunity to present further qualifications or to indicate that you have nothing to add. So, if you feel that a significant qualification or characteristic has been overlooked, it is proper to point it out in a sentence or so. Do not compliment the board on the thoroughness of their examination – they have been sketchy, and you know it. If you wish, merely say, "No thank you, I have nothing further to add." This is a point where you can "talk yourself out" of a good impression or fail to present an important bit of information. Remember, *you close the interview yourself.*

The chairman will then say, "That is all, Mr. _____, thank you." Do not be startled; the interview is over, and quicker than you think. Thank him, gather your belongings and take your leave. Save your sigh of relief for the other side of the door.

How to put your best foot forward

Throughout this entire process, you may feel that the board individually and collectively is trying to pierce your defenses, seek out your hidden weaknesses and embarrass and confuse you. Actually, this is not true. They are obliged to make an appraisal of your qualifications for the job you are seeking, and they want to see you in your best light. Remember, they must interview all candidates and a non-cooperative candidate may become a failure in spite of their best efforts to bring out his qualifications. Here are 15 suggestions that will help you:

1) Be natural – Keep your attitude confident, not cocky

If you are not confident that you can do the job, do not expect the board to be. Do not apologize for your weaknesses, try to bring out your strong points. The board is interested in a positive, not negative, presentation. Cockiness will antagonize any board member and make him wonder if you are covering up a weakness by a false show of strength.

2) Get comfortable, but don't lounge or sprawl

Sit erectly but not stiffly. A careless posture may lead the board to conclude that you are careless in other things, or at least that you are not impressed by the importance of the occasion. Either conclusion is natural, even if incorrect. Do not fuss with your clothing, a pencil or an ashtray. Your hands may occasionally be useful to emphasize a point; do not let them become a point of distraction.

3) Do not wisecrack or make small talk

This is a serious situation, and your attitude should show that you consider it as such. Further, the time of the board is limited – they do not want to waste it, and neither should you.

4) Do not exaggerate your experience or abilities
In the first place, from information in the application or other interviews and sources, the board may know more about you than you think. Secondly, you probably will not get away with it. An experienced board is rather adept at spotting such a situation, so do not take the chance.

5) If you know a board member, do not make a point of it, yet do not hide it
Certainly you are not fooling him, and probably not the other members of the board. Do not try to take advantage of your acquaintanceship – it will probably do you little good.

6) Do not dominate the interview
Let the board do that. They will give you the clues – do not assume that you have to do all the talking. Realize that the board has a number of questions to ask you, and do not try to take up all the interview time by showing off your extensive knowledge of the answer to the first one.

7) Be attentive
You only have 20 minutes or so, and you should keep your attention at its sharpest throughout. When a member is addressing a problem or question to you, give him your undivided attention. Address your reply principally to him, but do not exclude the other board members.

8) Do not interrupt
A board member may be stating a problem for you to analyze. He will ask you a question when the time comes. Let him state the problem, and wait for the question.

9) Make sure you understand the question
Do not try to answer until you are sure what the question is. If it is not clear, restate it in your own words or ask the board member to clarify it for you. However, do not haggle about minor elements.

10) Reply promptly but not hastily
A common entry on oral board rating sheets is "candidate responded readily," or "candidate hesitated in replies." Respond as promptly and quickly as you can, but do not jump to a hasty, ill-considered answer.

11) Do not be peremptory in your answers
A brief answer is proper – but do not fire your answer back. That is a losing game from your point of view. The board member can probably ask questions much faster than you can answer them.

12) Do not try to create the answer you think the board member wants
He is interested in what kind of mind you have and how it works – not in playing games. Furthermore, he can usually spot this practice and will actually grade you down on it.

13) Do not switch sides in your reply merely to agree with a board member
Frequently, a member will take a contrary position merely to draw you out and to see if you are willing and able to defend your point of view. Do not start a debate, yet do not surrender a good position. If a position is worth taking, it is worth defending.

14) Do not be afraid to admit an error in judgment if you are shown to be wrong

The board knows that you are forced to reply without any opportunity for careful consideration. Your answer may be demonstrably wrong. If so, admit it and get on with the interview.

15) Do not dwell at length on your present job

The opening question may relate to your present assignment. Answer the question but do not go into an extended discussion. You are being examined for a *new* job, not your present one. As a matter of fact, try to phrase ALL your answers in terms of the job for which you are being examined.

Basis of Rating

Probably you will forget most of these "do's" and "don'ts" when you walk into the oral interview room. Even remembering them all will not ensure you a passing grade. Perhaps you did not have the qualifications in the first place. But remembering them will help you to put your best foot forward, without treading on the toes of the board members.

Rumor and popular opinion to the contrary notwithstanding, an oral board wants you to make the best appearance possible. They know you are under pressure – but they also want to see how you respond to it as a guide to what your reaction would be under the pressures of the job you seek. They will be influenced by the degree of poise you display, the personal traits you show and the manner in which you respond.

ABOUT THIS BOOK

This book contains tests divided into Examination Sections. Go through each test, answering every question in the margin. We have also attached a sample answer sheet at the back of the book that can be removed and used. At the end of each test look at the answer key and check your answers. On the ones you got wrong, look at the right answer choice and learn. Do not fill in the answers first. Do not memorize the questions and answers, but understand the answer and principles involved. On your test, the questions will likely be different from the samples. Questions are changed and new ones added. If you understand these past questions you should have success with any changes that arise. Tests may consist of several types of questions. We have additional books on each subject should more study be advisable or necessary for you. Finally, the more you study, the better prepared you will be. This book is intended to be the last thing you study before you walk into the examination room. Prior study of relevant texts is also recommended. NLC publishes some of these in our Fundamental Series. Knowledge and good sense are important factors in passing your exam. Good luck also helps. So now study this Passbook, absorb the material contained within and take that knowledge into the examination. Then do your best to pass that exam.

EXAMINATION SECTION

EXAMINATION SECTION
TEST 1

DIRECTIONS: Each question or incomplete statement is followed by several suggested answers or completions. Select the one that BEST answers the question or completes the statement. *PRINT THE LETTER OF THE CORRECT ANSWER IN TEE SPACE AT THE RIGHT.*

1. Police Communications Technicians must connect the caller to Transit Police when an incident occurs on a subway train or in the subway station.
   Which one of the following calls should be reported to Transit Police?

   A. The newsstand outside the entrance to the 86th Street subway was just robbed, and the suspects fled down the street.
   B. Soon after James Pike left the Columbus Circle subway station, his chain was snatched on the street corner.
   C. While traveling to work on the *D* line subway train, John Smith was mugged.
   D. A noisy group of school children have just come out of the Times Square subway station and are now annoying passersby on the street.

1.____

Question 2.

DIRECTIONS: Question 2 is to be answered SOLELY on the basis of the following information.
   When a Police Communications Technician is notified by patrol cars that they are in a vehicular pursuit, the dispatcher should obtain the following in the order given:
   I. Location of pursuit
   II. Type of vehicle, color of vehicle, and direction of travel
   III. Nature of offense
   IV. License plate number and state
   V. Number of occupant(s) in vehicle
   VI. Identity of the patrol car in pursuit

2. Police Communications Dispatcher Johnson is working the 26th Division when an unknown patrol car announces via car radio that he is in pursuit of a white 1986 Cadillac traveling north on Vanbrunt Street from Ainsley Place. Dispatcher Johnson then asks the pursuing patrol car, *What is the car wanted for?* The Officer replies, *The car is wanted for a hit and run.*
   What information should Dispatcher Johnson obtain NEXT?

   A. The number of occupant(s) in the vehicle
   B. Location of pursuit
   C. License plate number and state
   D. Identity of the patrol car in pursuit

2.____

Question 3.

DIRECTIONS: Question 3 is to be answered SOLELY on the basis of the following information.

Robbery - involves the unlawful taking of property from a person by force or attempted use of immediate force.

Robbery in Progress - crime is occurring at the time the call came into 911, 5 minutes in the past or when suspects are still in the area.

3. Which of the following situations would be considered a ROBBERY IN PROGRESS? 3.____

    A. Female calls 911 stating that she has just arrived home and found her apartment has been robbed.
    B. Male calls 911 stating that he just discovered that someone picked his pocket.
    C. Female calls 911 stating that she saw a man grab an elderly woman's purse.
    D. Child calls 911 stating that some man is beating up his mother and is trying to take her purse.

4. On June 20, 2007 at 6:30 P.M., Police Communications Technician White receives a call from an anonymous complainant stating the following facts: 4.____
Incident: Male with a gun sitting in a blue car
Location of Incident: In front of 185 Hall St.
Description of Suspect: Male, Black, bald, approximately 25 years old, dressed in red

Dispatcher White needs to be accurate and clear when transferring above information to the police dispatcher. Which one of the following expresses the above information MOST clearly and accurately?

    A. On June 20, 2007 at 6:30 P.M., a call was received stating that a bald man, dressed in red, was in front of 185 Hall St. A black male, approximately 25 years old, is sitting in a blue car holding a gun.
    B. A call was received on June 20, 2007. at 6:30 P.M. stating that a bald black male, approximately 25 years old, who is dressed in red, is armed with a gun sitting in a blue car in front of 185 Hall St.
    C. A call was received on June 20, 2007 at 6:30 P.M. Sitting in a blue car in front of 185 Hall St. is a Black male, approximately 25 years old. Dressed in red with a bald head, a man is armed with a gun.
    D. A call was received stating that in front of 185 Hall St., a bald male, approximately 25 years old, dressed in red, is sitting in a blue car. A Black male is armed with a gun at 6:30 P.M. on June 20, 2007.

5. Police Communications Technician Dozier receives a call from a female who has just witnessed the following: 5.____
Incident: White female police officer being assaulted
Location of Incident: Surf Avenue and West 30th Street, in front of a candy store
Description of Suspectp; Hispanic female wearing a green dress, possibly armed with a gun

Dispatcher Dozier is about to relay the information to the dispatcher.
Which one of the following expresses the above information MOST clearly and accurately?

    A. A call was received from a female on Surf Avenue and West 30th Street stating that a white female police officer is being assaulted by a Hispanic female wearing a green dress. She is possibly armed with a gun in front of a candy store.
    B. In front of a candy store at Surf Avenue and West 30th Street, a call was received from a female stating that a white female police officer is being assaulted by a Hispanic female wearing a green dress. She is possibly armed with a gun.

C. A call was received from a female stating that at the corner of Surf Avenue and West 30th Street in front of a candy store, there is a white female police officer being assaulted. The suspect is a Hispanic female wearing a green dress, who is possibly armed with a gun.
D. A call was received from a female stating that at the corner of West 30th Street and Surf Avenue, there is a white female police officer in front of a candy store being assaulted. She is wearing a green dress. The Hispanic female is possibly armed with a gun.

Questions 6-8.

DIRECTIONS: Questions 6 through 8 are to be answered SOLELY on the basis of the following passage.

At 10:35 A.M., Police Communications Technician Ross receives a second call from Mrs. Smith who is very upset because she has been waiting for the police and an ambulance since her first call, one hour ago. Mrs. Smith was mugged, and in resisting the attack, her nose was broken. The location of the incident is the uptown side of the subway station for the IND #2 train located at Jay Street and Borough Hall. Operator Ross advises Mrs. Smith to hold on and that she will check the status of her complaint. Operator Ross calls the Emergency Medical Service (EMS) and connects Mrs. Smith to the EMS operator. The EMS operator informs Mrs. Smith that an ambulance is coming from a far distance away and will be at the location at approximately 11:03 A.M. Operator Ross then calls the Transit Authority Police Department (TAPD). The TAPD received Mrs. Smith's first call at 9:37 A.M., and police arrived at location at 9:46 M. However, the police arrived at the downtown side of the subway station for the IND #3 train. TAPD informs Operator Ross that a police car will arrive at the correct location as soon as possible.

6. What is the CLOSEST approximate time that Mrs. Smith made her first call for help? _____ A.M.

    A. 9:35   B. 9:46   C. 10:35   D. 11:03 .

7. The ambulance was delayed because

    A. the ambulance responded to the downtown side of the subway station for the IND #2 train
    B. EMS never received Mrs. Smith's request for an ambulance
    C. a broken nose is not a priority request for an ambulance
    D. the ambulance was coming from a far distance

8. There was a delay in TAPD response to the crime scene because TAPD

    A. was coming from a far distance
    B. responded on the uptown side of the subway station for the IND #2 train
    C. was waiting for the -Police Department to respond first
    D. responded on the downtown side of the subway station for the IND #3 train

9. Extreme care must be taken when assigning solo cars (one police officer in a vehicle) to incidents. If anything in the job indicates that the job may be a potentially violent situation, a solo car should not be assigned.
   In which one of the following incidents should a Police Communications Technician assign a solo car?
   A

   A. disorderly male carrying a knife
   B. house that was broken into two days ago
   C. suspiciously occupied auto
   D. group of rowdy teenagers throwing beer bottles at passersbys

Question 10.

DIRECTIONS: Question 10 is to be answered SOLELY on the basis of the following information.

On the Police Communications Technician's screen, the following incidents appear which were called in at the same time:
   I. Caller states that she is looking out her 10th floor window and sees a man sleeping on the street in front of her home at Crescent Street and 4th Avenue.
   II. Caller states that he was driving down the block of Crescent Street between 3rd and 4th Avenues and just witnessed a man being beaten and mugged. The caller thinks that the victim is unconscious.
   III. Caller states there is a car accident at Crescent Street and 3rd Avenue, and one of the passengers suffered a broken arm.

10. Which of the above should the operator MOST likely consider as the same incident?

    A. I and II   B. II and III
    C. I and III   D. I, II, and III

11. Police Communications Operator Raymond receives a call regarding a rape and obtains the following information:
    Time of Rape: 10:35 P.M.
    Place of Rape: Sam's Laundromat, 200 Melrose Avenue
    Victim: Joan McGraw
    Crime: Rape
    Suspect: Male, Hispanic, carrying a gun
    Operator Raymond is about to enter the incident into the computer.
    Which one of the following expresses the above information MOST clearly and accurately?

    A. At 10:35 P.M., Joan McGraw was raped in Sam's Laundromat, located at 200 Melrose Avenue, by a Hispanic male carrying a gun.
    B. A Hispanic male was carrying a gun at 10:35 P.M. Joan McGraw was raped in Sam's Laundromat located at 200 Melrose Avenue.
    C. Carrying a gun, Joan McGraw was raped by a Hispanic male. This occurred in Sam's Laundromat located at 200 Melrose Avenue at 10:35 P.M.
    D. At 10:35 P.M., Joan McGraw was raped by a Hispanic male carrying a gun. Sam's Laundromat is located at 200 Melrose Avenue.

12. Police Communications Dispatcher Gold receives a call concerning a disorderly male in a local drug store. He obtains the following information:
    Place of Occurrence: Rapid-Serve Drug Store
    Complainant: George Meyer
    Crime: Threatening gestures and abusive language
    Suspect: Male, white
    Action Taken: The suspect was removed from premises by the police.
    Dispatcher Gold is about to enter the incident into the computer.
    Which one of the following expresses the above information MOST clearly and accurately?

    A. George Meyer called the police because a white male was removed from the Rapid-Serve Drug Store. He was making threatening gestures and using abusive language.
    B. George Meyer called the police and was removed from the Rapid-Serve Drug Store. A white male was making threatening gestures and using abusive language.
    C. At the Rapid-Serve Drug Store, a white male was making threatening gestures and using abusive language. George Meyer called the police and removed the suspect from the drug store.
    D. George Meyer called the police because a white male was making threatening gestures and using abusive language in the Rapid-Serve Drug Store. The suspect was removed from the drug store by the police.

12._____

Question 13.

DIRECTIONS: Question 13 is to be answered SOLELY on the basis of the following information.

When dispatching an incident involving a suspicious package, a Police Communications Technician should do the following in the order given:

    I. Assign a patrol car and Patrol Sergeant.
    II. Enter into the computer additional information received from assigned cars.
    III. Notify appropriate Emergency Assistance.
    IV. Notify the Bomb Squad.
    V. Notify the Duty Captain.

13. Police Communications Technician Berlin receives a call involving a suspicious package located on the corner of Gates Avenue and Blake Street. Dispatcher Berlin promptly assigns a patrol car and a Patrol Sergeant to the incident. Upon arrival, the Sergeant determines that there is a ticking sound coming from the box. The Sergeant immediately advises Dispatcher Berlin of the situation and tells Dispatcher Berlin to call the Fire Department and have them respond.
    What should Dispatcher Berlin to NEXT?

    A. Call the Fire Department.
    B. Notify the Bomb Squad.
    C. Enter additional information received from assigned cars into the computer.
    D. Notify the Duty Captain.

13._____

Questions 14-16.

DIRECTIONS: Questions 14 through 16 are to be answered SOLELY on the basis of the following passage.

Police Communications Technician Robbins receives a call at 5:15 P.M. from Mr. Adams reporting he witnessed a shooting in front of 230 Eagle Road. Mr. Adams, who lives at 234 Eagle Road, states he overheard two white males arguing with a Black man. He describes one white male as having blonde hair and wearing a black jacket with blue jeans, and the other white male as having brown hair and wearing a white jacket and blue jeans.

Mr. Adams recognized the Black man as John Rivers, the son of Mrs. Mary Rivers, who lives at 232 Eagle Road. At 5:10 P.M., the blonde male took a gun, shot John in the stomach, and dragged his body into the alleyway. The two males ran into the backyard of 240 Eagle Road and headed west on Randall Boulevard. Dispatcher Robbins connects Mr. Adams to the Emergency Medical Service. The Ambulance Receiving Operator processes the call at 5:25 P.M. and advises Mr. Adams that the next available ambulance will be sent.

14. Who was the eyewitness to the shooting?

    A. Dispatcher Robbins
    B. Mr. Adams
    C. Mrs. Rivers
    D. John Rivers

15. In front of what address was John Rivers shot? _____ Eagle Road.

    A. 230   B. 232   C. 234   D. 240

16. What is the description of the male who fired the gun? A male wearing a _____ jacket and blue jeans.

    A. white blonde-haired; white
    B. white brown-haired; black
    C. white blonde-haired; black
    D. Black brown-haired; white

17. A Police Communications Technician can have several calls for police response on their computer screen at one time. A dispatcher may have to determine which of the calls is the most serious and assign that one to the police first.
Which one of the following situations should a dispatcher assign to the police FIRST?

    A. A robbery which occurred two hours ago, and the suspects have fled the scene
    B. A suspicious man offering a child candy to get the child into his van at the time of the call
    C. A woman returns to her car and finds her left fender dented
    D. A group of youths playing cards in the hallway

18. The following information was obtained by Police Communications Technician Fried regarding a call of an auto accident with injuries:
    Date of Accident: March 7, 2007
    Place of Accident: 50 West 96th Street
    Time of Accident: 3:15 P.M.
    Drivers: Susan Green and Nancy White

Injured: Nancy White
Action Taken: Emergency Medical Services (EMS) Operator 600 was notified
Dispatcher Fried is about to enter the above information into the computer.
Which one of the following expresses the above information MOST clearly and accurately?

- A. At 50 West 96th Street, Susan Green and Nancy White had an auto accident resulting in an injury to Nancy White. EMS Operator 600 was notifed to send an ambulance at 3:15 P.M. on March 7, 2007.
- B. EMS Operator 600 was notified to send an ambulance to 50 West 96th Street due to an auto accident between Nancy White and Susan Green, who was injured on March 7, 2007 at 3:15 P.M.
- C. Susan Green and Nancy White were involved in an auto accident at 50 West 96th Street on March 7, 2007. At 3:15 P.M., EMS Operator 600 was notified to send an ambulance for Nancy White.
- D. On March 7, 2007 at 3:15 P.M., Susan Green and Nancy White were involved in an auto accident at 50 West 96th Street. EMS Operator 600 was notified to send an ambulance for Nancy White who was injured in the accident.

Questions 19-20.

DIRECTIONS: Questions 19 and 20 are to be answered SOLELY on the basis of the following information.

At the beginning of their tours, Police Communications Technicians need to call the precinct to find out what patrol cars are covering which sections of the precinct and which special assignment cars are being used. Special assignment cars are used instead of regular patrol cars when certain situations arise. Special assignment cars should be assigned before a patrol car when a call comes in that is related to the car's special assignment, regardless of what section the incident is occurring in. Otherwise, a regular patrol car should be assigned.

Police Communications Technician Tanner is assigned to the 83rd Precinct. He calls the precinct and determines the following patrol cars and special assignment cars are being used:

Patrol cars are assigned as follows:
  Patrol Car 83A - Covers Sections A, B, C
  Patrol Car 83D - Covers Sections D, E, F
  Patrol Car 83G - Covers Sections G, H, I

Special assignment cars are assigned as follows:
  83SP1 - Burglary Car
  83SP2 - Religious Establishment
  83SP8 - Anti-Crime (plainclothes officers)

19. Dispatcher Tanner receives a call located in the 83rd Precinct in *E* Section. Which car should be assigned?

    A. 83D   B. 83A   C. 83SP8   D. 83SP2

20. Dispatcher Tanner receives a call concerning a burglary in *B* Section. Which is the CORRECT car to be assigned?

    A. 83A   B. 83G   C. 83SP1   D. 83SP2

KEY (CORRECT ANSWERS)

1.	C	11.	A
2.	C	12.	D
3.	D	13.	C
4.	B	14.	B
5.	C	15.	A
6.	A	16.	C
7.	D	17.	B
8.	D	18.	D
9.	B	19.	A
10.	A	20.	C

TEST 2

DIRECTIONS: Each question or incomplete statement is followed by several suggested answers or completions. Select the one that BEST answers the question or completes the statement. *PRINT THE LETTER OF THE CORRECT ANSWER IN THE SPACE AT THE RIGHT.*

1. Police Communications Technician Daniel receives a call stating the following: 1.____
   Date and Time of Call: June 21, 2007 at 12:30 P.M.
   Incident: Shots being fired
   Location: The roof of a building, located between Moore Street and Bushwick Avenue, exact address unknown
   Suspect: Male
   Complainant: Mr. Bernard
   Comments: Mr. Bernard will be wearing a brown coat and will direct officers to location of the incident.

   Dispatcher Daniel is about to enter the information into the computer.
   Which one of the following expresses the above information MOST clearly and accurately?
   On June 21, 2007,

   A. at 12:30 P.M., Dispatcher Daniel receives a call from a complainant stating that a male is on a roof of a building with an unknown address firing a gun, and he is wearing a brown coat. The complainant, Mr. Bernard, will be in front of the building to direct the police to the exact location of the incident.
   B. a male is firing a gun from a roof, stated complainant Mr. Bernard to Dispatcher Daniel. This is at Moore Street and Bushwick Avenue. At 12:30 P.M., the caller will be at the location to direct the police to the building where the male is firing the gun. He is wearing a brown coat.
   C. at 12:30 P.M., Dispatcher Daniel receives a call from a complainant, Mr. Bernard, who states that at a building with an unknown address, located between Moore Street and Bushwick Avenue, a male is firing a gun from a roof. Mr. Bernard will be at the location wearing a brown coat to direct the police to the exact building.
   D. Dispatcher Daniel receives a call from a complainant, Mr. Bernard, who is calling from a building with an unknown address. He informs Dispatcher Daniel that a male is firing a gun from a roof of a building between Moore Street and Bushwick Avenue. At 12:30 P.M., Mr. Bernard will be wearing a brown coat to direct the police to the incident.

Questions 2-4.

DIRECTIONS: Questions 2 through 4 are to be answered SOLELY on the basis of the following passage.

Mrs. Arroyo returns from work one evening to find her door open and loud noise coming from her apartment. She peeks through the crack of the door and sees a white male moving rapidly through her apartment wearing blue jeans and a pink T-shirt. She runs to the nearest public telephone and dials 911. Police Communications Technician Ms. Lopez takes the call. Mrs. Arroyo informs Operator Lopez that there is a strange man in her apartment. The operator asks the caller for her address, apartment number, name, and telephone number, and then puts Mrs. Arroyo on hold. Operator Lopez enters the address in the computer and, realizing it is a high priority call, tries to notify the Radio Dispatcher directly by depressing the *hotline* button.

The Radio Dispatcher does not respond, and Operator Lopez realizes the *hotline* button is not working. The operator then continues to enter the rest of the information into the computer and notifies the caller that the police will respond. Operator Lopez then walks into the dispatcher's room to make sure the dispatcher received the information entered into the computer, and then notifies the supervisor of her malfunctioning equipment.

2. The operator notified her supervisor because

    A. the suspect was still in the apartment
    B. the *hotline* button was not working
    C. she could not enter the address in the computer
    D. it was a high priority call

3. What was the FIRST action the operator took after putting the complainant on hold?

    A. Entered the caller's telephone number and name in the computer.
    B. Walked into the dispatcher's room.
    C. Entered the caller's address into the computer.
    D. Tried to notify the Radio Dispatcher by depressing the *hotline* button.

4. Operator Lopez depressed the *hotline* button

    A. to check if the *hotline* button was working properly
    B. because it was a high priority call
    C. to make sure the dispatcher received the information entered into the computer
    D. because the computer was not working properly

Question 5.

DIRECTIONS: Question 5 is to be answered SOLELY on the basis of the following information.

A Police Communications Technician occasionally receives calls from persons making threats against public officials, visiting dignitaries, or members of the Police Department. When this occurs, the Dispatcher should do the following in the order given:

    I. Obtain details of the threat
       (A) Who is being threatened and how
       (B) When it is going to happen
    II. Attempt to determine the sex and ethnicity of the caller
    III. Try to obtain the identity, address, and telephone number of the caller
    IV. Notify the supervisor

5. Police Communications Operator Frye receives a call and obtains from the caller that he is going to shoot the mayor on Election Day. Operator Frye determine the caller to be a male with a heavy Hispanic accent. Operator Frye asks the male for his name, address, and phone number. The caller does not respond and hangs up.
What should Operator Frye do NEXT?

    A. Obtain details of the threats.
    B. Determine the sex and ethnicity of the caller.
    C. Obtain the identity, address, and phone number of the caller.
    D. Notify the supervisor.

Question 6.

DIRECTIONS: Question 6 is to be answered SOLELY on the basis of the following information.

A Police Communications Technician will call back complainants only under the following conditions:
1. Dispatcher needs clarification of information previously received from the complainant and/or
2. To notify the complainant that police need to gain entry to the location of the incident.

6. In which one of the following situations should a Police Communications Technician call back the complainant?

    A. While responding to an assigned incident, Patrol Car 79A gets a flat tire. Patrol Car 79A radios the dispatcher and advises the dispatcher to call the complainant and notify the complainant that there will be a delay in police response.
    B. Patrol Car 83B is assigned to an incident that occurred approximately 30 minutes ago. Patrol Car 83B advises the dispatcher that he is coming from a far distance and the dispatcher should call the complainant to find out which is the best way to get to the incident location.
    C. Patrol Car 66B is on the scene of an incident and is having a problem gaining entry into the building. Patrol Car 66B asks the dispatcher to call the complainant and ask him to meet the police officers from the patrol car outside the building.
    D. Patrol Car 90B is assigned to a burglary that occurred in the complainant's private home. It is raining heavily outside, so Patrol Car 90B asks the dispatcher to call and request the complainant to meet the police by the patrol car.

6._____

7. Police Communications Dispatcher Blake receives a call reporting a bank robbery and obtains the following information:

    Time of Robbery: 11:30 A.M.
    Place of Robbery: Fidelity Bank
    Crime: Bank Robbery
    Suspect: Male, white, wearing blue jeans, blue jacket, carrying a brown bag
    Witness: Susan Lane of 731 Madison Avenue

    Dispatcher Blake is about to inform his supervisor of the facts concerning the bank robbery.
    Which one of the following expresses the above information MOST clearly and accurately?

    A. At 11:30 A.M., the Fidelity Bank was robbed. Susan Lane lives at 731 Madison Avenue. The witness saw a white male wearing blue jeans, a blue jacket, and carrying a brown bag.
    B. Susan Lane of 731 Madison Avenue witnessed the robbery of Fidelity Bank at 11:30 A.M. The suspect is a white male and was wearing blue jeans, a blue jacket, and carrying a brown bag.
    C. Wearing blue jeans, a blue jacket, and carrying a brown bag, Susan Lane of 731 Madison Avenue saw a white male robbing the Fidelity Bank. The robbery was witnessed at 11:30 A.M.

7._____

D. At 11:30 A.M., Susan Lane of 731 Madison Avenue witnessed the robbery of the Fidelity Bank. A white male wore blue jeans, a blue jacket, and carried a brown bag.

8. Police Communications Technician Levine receives an incident for dispatch containing the following information:

   Incident: A female being beaten
   Location: In front of 385 Wall Street
   Victim: White female
   Suspect: White, male, wearing a grey shirt, possibly concealing a gun underneath his shirt

   Dispatcher Levine is about to relay this information to the patrol car.
   Which one of the following expresses the above information MOST clearly and accurately?

   A. A white female is being beaten by a white male wearing a grey shirt, who is possibly concealing a gun underneath his shirt. This is occurring in front of 385 Wall Street.
   B. A white male is beating a white female wearing a grey shirt. He is possibly concealing a gun underneath his shirt in front of 385 Wall Street.
   C. A female is being beaten in front of 385 Wall Street. A white male is possibly concealing a gun underneath his shirt. She is white, and the suspect is wearing a grey shirt.
   D. In front of 385 Wall Street, a white female is being beaten by a suspect, possibly concealing a gun underneath his shirt. A white male is wearing a grey shirt.

8.____

Questions 9-11.

DIRECTIONS: Questions 9 through 11 are to be answered SOLELY on the basis of the following passage.

Police Communications Technician John Clove receives a call from a Social Worker, Mrs. Norma Harris of Presbyterian Hospital, who states there is a 16-year-old teenager on the other line, speaking to Dr. Samuel Johnson, a psychologist at the hospital. The teenager is threatening suicide and claims that she is an out-patient, but refuses to give her name, address, or telephone number. She further states that the teenager took 100 pills of valium and is experiencing dizziness, numbness of the lips, and heart palpitations. The teenager tells Dr. Johnson that she wants to die because her boyfriend left her because she is pregnant.

Dr. Johnson is keeping her on the line persuading her to give her name, telephone number, and address. The Social Worker asks the dispatcher to trace the call. The dispatcher puts the caller on hold and informs his supervisor, Mrs. Ross, of the incident. The supervisor contacts Telephone Technician Mr. Ralph Taylor. Mr. Taylor contacts the telephone company and speaks to Supervisor Wallace, asking him to trace the call between Dr. Johnson and the teenager. After approximately 10 minutes, the dispatcher gets back to the Social Worker and informs her that the call is being traced.

9. Why did the Social Worker call Dispatcher Clove?

   A. A teenager is threatening suicide.
   B. Mrs. Ross took 100 pills of valium.

9.____

C. Dr. Johnson felt dizzy, numbness of the lips, and heart palpitations.
D. An unmarried teenager is pregnant.

10. Who did Mr. Clove notify FIRST? 10.____

    A. Mrs. Norma Harris
    B. Dr. Samuel Johnson
    C. Mr. Wallace
    D. Mrs. Ross

11. The conversation between which two individuals is being traced? 11.____

    A. Mrs. Norma Harris and the 16-year-old teenager
    B. The Telephone Technician and Telephone Company Supervisor
    C. Dr. Johnson and the 16-year-old teenager
    D. The dispatcher and the Hospital Social Worker

Question 12.

DIRECTIONS: Question 12 is to be answered SOLELY on the basis of the following information.

On the Police Communications Technician's screen, the following incidents appear which were called in at the same time by three different callers:

   I. A fight is occurring at 265 Hall Street between Myrtle and Willoughby Ave. The fight started in Apartment 3C, and the two men are now fighting in the street.
   II. A fight took place between a security guard and a suspected shoplifter in a store at Hall St. and Willoughby Ave. The security guard is holding the suspect in the security office.
   III. A fight is occurring between two white males on the street near the corner of Hall Street and Myrtle Ave. One of the males has a baseball bat.

12. Which of the above should a Police Communications Technician MOST likely consider as the same incident? 12.____

    A. I and II
    B. II and III
    C. I and III
    D. I, II, and III

Questions 13-15.

DIRECTIONS: Questions 13 through 15 are to be answered SOLELY on the basis of the following passage.

Police Communications Technician Flood receives a call from Mr. Michael Watkins, Program Director for *Meals on Wheels,* a program that delivers food to elderly people who cannot leave their home. Mr. Watkins states he received a call from Rochelle Berger, whose elderly aunt, Estelle Sims, is a client of his. Rochelle Berger informed Mr. Watkins that she has just received a call from her aunt's neighbor, Sally Bowles, who told her that her aunt has not eaten in several days and is in need of medical attention.

After questioning Mr. Watkins, Dispatcher Flood is informed that Estelle Sims lives at 300 79th Street in Apartment 6K, and her telephone number is 686-4527; Sally Bowles lives in Apartment 6H, and her telephone number is 678-2456. Mr. Watkins further advises that if there is difficulty getting into Estelle Sims' apartment, to ring Sally Bowies' bell and she will let you in. Mr. Watkins gives his phone number as 776-0451, and Rochelle Berger's phone number is 291-7287. Dispatcher Flood advises Mr. Watkins that the appropriate medical assistance will be sent.

13. Who did Sally Bowles notify that her neighbor needed medical attention?

    A. Dispatcher Flood
    B. Michael Watkins
    C. Rochelle Berger
    D. Estelle Sims

14. If the responding medical personnel are unable to get into Apartment 6K, they should speak to

    A. Rochelle Berger
    B. Sally Bowles
    C. Dispatcher Flood
    D. Michael Watkins

15. Whose telephone number is 686-4527?

    A. Michael Watkins
    B. Estelle Sims
    C. Sally Bowles
    D. Rochelle Berger

16. Police Communications Technicians often receive calls regarding incidents where a response from the Fire Department may be necessary.
    In which one of the following situations would a request from the dispatcher for the Fire Department to respond be MOST critical?
    A(n)

    A. fire hydrant has been opened by children on a hot August afternoon
    B. abandoned auto is parked in front of a fire hydrant
    C. neighbor's cat has climbed up a tree and is stuck
    D. excited woman smells smoke coming from the floor below

Question 17.

DIRECTIONS: Question 17 is to be answered SOLELY on the basis of the following information.

When a patrol car confirms that a murder has taken place, the Police Communications Technician should notify the following people in the order given:
   I. Patrol Sergeant
   II. Dispatching Supervisor
   III. Operations Unit
   IV. Crime Scene Unit
   V. Precinct Detective Unit
   VI. Duty Captain

17. Police Communications Technician Rodger assigns a patrol car to investigate a man who was shot and killed. The patrol car arrives on the scene and confirms that a murder has taken place. The Patrol Sergeant hears what has happened on his police radio and informs Dispatcher Rodger that he is going to respond to the scene. The Dispatching Supervisor walks over to Dispatcher Rodger and is informed of the situation.
    Who should Dispatcher Rodger notify NEXT?

    A. Operations Unit
    B. Patrol Sergeant
    C. Precinct Detective Unit
    D. Crime Scene Unit

18. Police Communications Technician Peterson receives a call from a woman inside the subway station reporting that her purse has just been snatched. Dispatcher Peterson obtained the following information relating to the crime:
Place of Occurrence: E. 42nd Street and Times Square
Time of Occurrence: 5:00 P.M.
Crime: Purse Snatched
Victim: Thelma Johnson
Description of Suspect: Black, female, brown hair, blue jeans, red T-shirt
Dispatcher Peterson is about to relay the information to the Transit Authority Police Dispatcher.
Which one of the following expresses the above information MOST clearly and accurately?

   A. At 5:00 P.M., a brown-haired Black woman snatched a purse inside the subway station at E. 42nd Street and Times Square belonging to Thelma Johnson. She was wearing blue jeans and a red T-shirt.
   B. A purse was snatched from Thelma Johnson by a woman with brown hair in the subway station at 5:00 P.M. A Black female was wearing blue jeans and a red T-shirt at E. 42nd Street and Times Square.
   C. At 5:00 P.M., Thelma Johnson's purse was snatched inside the subway station at E. 42nd Street and Times Square. The suspect is a Black female with brown hair who is wearing blue jeans and a red T-shirt.
   D. Thelma Johnson reported at 5:00 P.M. her purse was snatched. In the subway station at E. 42nd Street and Times Square, a Black female with brown hair was wearing blue jeans and a red T-shirt.

19. Police Communications Technician Hopkins receives a call of an assault and obtains the following information concerning the incident:
Place of Occurrence: Times Square
Time of Occurrence: 3:15 A.M.
Victim: Peter Polk
Victim's Address: 50 E. 60 Street
Suspect: Male, Hispanic, 5'6", 140 lbs., dressed in black
Injury: Broken nose
Action Taken: Victim transported to St. Luke's Hospital
Dispatcher Hopkins is about to enter the job into the computer system.
Which one of the following expresses the above information MOST clearly and accurately?

   A. At 3:15 A.M., Peter Polk was assaulted in Times Square by a Hispanic male, 5'6", 140 lbs., dressed in black, suffering a broken nose. Mr. Polk lives at 50 E. 69 Street and was transported to St. Luke's Hospital.
   B. At 3:15 A.M., Peter Polk was assaulted in Times Square by a Hispanic male, 5'6", 140 lbs., dressed in black, who lives at 50 E. 69 Street. Mr. Polk suffered a broken nose and was transported to St. Luke's Hospital.
   C. Peter Polk, who lives at 50 E. 69 Street, was assaulted at 3:15 A.M. in Times Square by a Hispanic male, 5'6", 140 lbs., dressed in black. Mr. Polk suffered a broken nose and was transported to St. Luke's Hospital.
   D. Living at 50 E. 69 Street, Mr. Polk suffered a broken nose and was transported to St. Luke's Hospital. At 3:15 A.M., Mr. Polk was assaulted by a Hispanic male, 5'6", 140 lbs., who was dressed in black.

20. A Police Communications Technician is required to determine which situations called in to 911 require police assistance and which calls require non-emergency assistance. Which one of the following calls should a dispatcher MOST likely refer to non-emergency assistance?

   A. Mr. Moss threatens the owner of Deluxe Deli with bodily harm for giving him incorrect change of twenty dollars.
   B. The manager refuses to take back Mrs. Thompson's defective toaster because she doesn't have a receipt. Mrs. Thompson leaves the store.
   C. Mrs. Frank is having a violent argument with the manager of Donna's Dress Shop because he is refusing to exchange a dress she recently purchased.
   D. The manager of Metro Supermarket refuses to take back a stale loaf of bread, so the consumer punches him in the face.

KEY (CORRECT ANSWERS)

1.	C	11.	C
2.	B	12.	C
3.	C	13.	C
4.	B	14.	B
5.	D	15.	B
6.	C	16.	D
7.	B	17.	A
8.	A	18.	C
9.	A	19.	C
10.	D	20.	B

EXAMINATION SECTION
TEST 1

DIRECTIONS: Each question or incomplete statement is followed by several suggested answers or completions. Select the one that BEST answers the question or completes the statement. *PRINT THE LETTER OF THE CORRECT ANSWER IN THE SPACE AT THE RIGHT.*

Questions 1-3.

DIRECTIONS: Questions 1 through 3 are to be answered SOLELY on the basis of the following passage.

On May 15 at 10:15 A.M., Mr. Price was returning to his home at 220 Kings Walk when he discovered two of his neighbor's apartment doors slightly opened. One neighbor, Mrs. Kagan, who lives alone in Apartment 1C, was away on vacation. The other apartment, IB, is occupied by Martin and Ruth Stone, an elderly couple, who usually take a walk everyday at 10:00 A.M. Fearing a robbery might be taking place, Mr. Price runs downstairs to Mr. White in Apartment BI to call the police. Police Communications Technician Johnson received the call at 10:20 A.M. Mr. Price gave his address and stated that two apartments were possibly being burglarized. Communications Technician Johnson verified the address in the computer and then asked Mr. Price for descriptions of the suspects. He explained that he had not seen anyone, but he believed that they were still inside the building. Communications Technician Johnson immediately notified the dispatcher who assigned two patrol cars at 10:25 A.M., while Mr. Price was still on the phone. Communications Technician Johnson told Mr. Price that the police were responding to the location.

1. Who called Communications Technician Johnson?   1.____
   A. Mrs. Kagan   B. Mr. White
   C. Mrs. Stone   D. Mr. Price

2. What time did Communications Technician Johnson receive the call?   2.____
   _____ A.M.
   A. 10:00   B. 10:15   C. 10:20   D. 10:25

3. Which tenant was away on vacation?   3.____
   The tenant in Apartment
   A. 1C   B. IB   C. BI   D. ID

4. Dispatcher Watkins receives the following information regarding a complaint.   4.____
   Place of occurrence: St. James Park
   Complaint: Large group of intoxicated males throwing beer bottles and playing loud music
   Complainant: Oscar Aker
   Complainant's Address: 13 St. James Square, Apt. 2B
   Dispatcher Watkins is not certain if this incident should be reported to 911 or Mr. Aker's local precinct. Dispatcher Watkins is about to notify his supervisor of the call. Which one of the following expresses the above information MOST clearly and accurately?

A. Mr. Aker, who lives at 13 St. James Square, Apt. 2B, called to make a complaint of a large group of intoxicated males who are throwing beer bottles and playing loud music in St. James Park.
B. Mr. Aker, who lives at 13 St. James Square, called to complain about a large group of intoxicated males, in Apt. 2B. They are throwing beer bottles and playing loud music in St. James Park.
C. Mr. Aker of 13 St. James Square, Apt. 2B, called to complain about loud music. There were a large group of intoxicated males throwing beer bottles in St. James Park.
D. As a result of intoxicated males throwing beer bottles Mr. Aker of 13 St. James Square, Apt. 2B, called to complain. A large group was playing loud music in St. James Park.

5. Communications Operator Davis recorded the following information from a caller: 5.____
Crime: Rape
Time of Rape: 11:30 A.M.
Place of Rape: Ralph's Dress Shop, 200 Lexington
Avenue Victim: Linda Castro - employee at Ralph's Dress Shop
Description of Suspect: Male, white
Weapon: Knife

Communications Operator Davis needs to be clear and accurate when relaying information to the patrol car. Which one of the following expresses the above information MOST clearly and accurately?

A. Linda Castro was at 200 Lexington Avenue when she was raped at knife point by a white male. At 11:30 A.M., she is an employee of Ralph's Dress Shop.
B. At 11:30 A.M., Linda Castro reported that she was working in Ralph's Dress Shop located at 200 Lexington Avenue. A white male raped her while she was working at knife point.
C. Linda Castro, an employee of Ralph's Dress Shop, located at 200 Lexington Avenue, reported that at 11:30 A.M. a white male raped her at knife point in the dress shop.
D. At 11:30 A.M., a white male pointed a knife at Linda Castro. He raped an employee of Ralph's Dress Shop, which is located at 200 Lexington Avenue.

Question 6.

DIRECTIONS: Question 6 is to be answered SOLELY on the basis of the following information.

Police Communications Technicians frequently receive low priority calls, which are calls that do not require an immediate police response. When a low priority call is received, the Police Communications Technician should transfer the caller to a tape-recorded message which states *there will be a delay in police response.*

6. Police Communications Technicians should transfer to the low priority taped message a 6.____
call reporting a

A. hubcap missing from an auto
B. child has just swallowed poison

C. group of youths fighting with knives
D. woman being assaulted

Questions 7-9.

DIRECTIONS: Questions 7 through 9 are to be answered SOLELY on the basis of the following passage.

On Tuesday, March 20 at 11:55 P.M., Dispatcher Uzel receives a call from a female stating that she immediately needs the police. The dispatcher asks the caller for her address. The excited female answers, *I can not think of it right now.* The dispatcher tries to calm down the caller. At this point, the female caller tells the dispatcher that her address is 1934 Bedford Avenue. The caller then realizes that 1934 Bedford Avenue is her mother's address and gives her address as 3455 Bedford Avenue. Dispatcher Uzel enters the address into the computer and tells the caller that the cross streets are Myrtle and Willoughby Avenues. The caller answers, *I don't live near Willoughby Avenue.* The dispatcher repeats her address at 3455 Bedford Avenue. Then the female states that her name is Linda Harris and her correct address is 5534 Bedford Avenue. Dispatcher Uzel enters the new address into the computer and determines the cross streets to be Utica Avenue and Kings Highway. The caller agrees that these are the cross streets where she lives.

7. What is the caller's CORRECT address?

   A. Unknown
   C. 3455 Bedford Avenue
   B. 1934 Bedford Avenue
   D. 5534 Bedford Avenue

8. What are the cross streets of the correct address?

   A. Myrtle Avenue and Willoughby Avenue
   B. Utica Avenue and Kings Highway
   C. Bedford Avenue and Myrtle Avenue
   D. Utica Avenue and Willoughby Avenue

9. Why did the female caller telephone Dispatcher Uzel?

   A. She needed the cross streets for her address.
   B. Her mother needed assistance.
   C. The purpose of the call was not mentioned.
   D. She did not know where she lived.

Question 10.

DIRECTIONS: Question 10 is to be answered SOLELY on the basis of the following information.

When performing vehicle license plate checks, Operators should do the following in the order given:
   I. Request the license plate in question.
   II. Repeat the license plate back to the patrol car officers.
   III. Check the license plate locally in the computer.
   IV. Advise the patrol car officers of the results of the local check.
   V. Check the license plate nationally in the computer.
   VI. Advise the patrol car officers of the results of the nationwide check.

10. Operator Johnson gets a request from a patrol car officer for a license plate check on a suspicious car. The patrol car officer tells Operator Johnson that the license plate number is XYZ-843, which Operator Johnson repeats back to the patrol car officer. Operator Johnson checks the license plate locally and determines that the car was stolen in the New York City area.
    What should Operator Johnson do NEXT?

    A. Repeat the license plate back to patrol car officers.
    B. Check the license plate nationally.
    C. Advise the patrol car officers of the results of the local check.
    D. Advise the patrol ear officers of the results of the nationwide check.

11. Police Communications Technician Hughes receives a call from the owner of The Diamond Dome Jewelry Store, reporting a robbery. He obtains the following information from the caller:

    Place of Occurrence: The Diamond Dome Jewelry Store, 10 Exchange Place
    Time of Occurrence: 10:00 A.M.
    Crime: Robbery of a $50,000 diamond ring
    Victim: Clayton Pelt, owner of The Diamond Dome Jewelry Store
    Description of Suspect: Male, white, black hair, blue suit and gray shirt
    Weapon: Gun

    Communications Technician Hughes is about to relay the information to the dispatcher. Which one of the following expresses the above information MOST clearly and accurately?

    A. Clayton Pelt reported that at 10:00 A.M. his store, The Diamond Dome Jewelry Store, was robbed at gunpoint. At 10 Exchange Place, a white male with black hair took a $50,000 diamond ring. He was wearing a blue suit and gray shirt.
    B. At 10:00 A.M., a black-haired male robbed a $50,000 diamond ring from The Diamond Dome Jewelry Store, which is owned by Clayton Pelt. A white male was wearing a blue suit and gray shirt and had a gun at 10 Exchange Place.
    C. At 10:00 A.M., Clayton Pelt, owner of The Diamond Dome Jewelry Store, which is located at 10 Exchange Place, was robbed of a $50,000 diamond ring at gunpoint. The suspect is a white male with black hair wearing a blue suit and gray shirt.
    D. In a robbery that occurred at gunpoint, a white male with black hair robbed The Diamond Dome Jewelry Store, which is located at 10 Exchange Place. Clayton Pelt, the owner who was robbed of a $50,000 diamond ring, said he was wearing a blue suit and a gray shirt at 10:00 A.M.

12. Dispatcher Sanders receives the following information from the computer: Place of Occurrence: Bushwick Housing Projects, rear of Building 12B

    Time of Occurrence: 6:00 P.M.
    Crime: Mugging
    Victim: Hispanic female
    Suspect: Unknown

    Dispatcher sanders is about to relay the information to the patrol car.
    Which one of the following expresses the above information MOST clearly and accurately?

A. In the rear of Building 12B, a Hispanic female was mugged. An unknown suspect was in the Bushwick Housing Projects at 6:00 P.M.
B. At 6:00 P.M., a Hispanic female was mugged by an unknown suspect in the rear of Building 12B, in the Bushwick Housing Projects.
C. At 6:00 P.M., a female is in the rear of Building 12B in the Bushwick Housing Projects. An unknown suspect mugged a Hispanic female.
D. A suspect's identity is unknown in the rear of Building 12B in the Bushwick Housing Project at 6:00 P.M. A Hispanic female was mugged.

Questions 13-15.

DIRECTIONS: Questions 13 through 15 are to be answered SOLELY on the basis of the following passage.

Dispatcher Clark, who is performing a 7:30 A.M. to 3:30 P.M. tour of duty, receives a call from Mrs. Gold. Mrs. Gold states there are four people selling drugs in front of Joe's Cleaners, located at the intersection of Main Street and Broadway. After checking the location in the computer, Dispatcher Clark asks the caller to give a description of each person. She gives the following descriptions: one white male wearing a yellow shirt, green pants, and red sneakers; one Hispanic male wearing a red and white shirt, black pants, and white sneakers; one black female wearing a green and red striped dress and red sandals; and one black male wearing a green shirt, yellow pants, and green sneakers. She also states that the Hispanic male, who is standing near a blue van, has the drugs inside a small black shoulder bag. She further states that she saw the black female hide a gun inside a brown paper bag and place it under a black car parked in front of Joe's Cleaners. The drug selling goes on everyday at various times. During the week, it occurs from 7 A.M. to 1 P.M. and from 5 P.M. to 12 A.M., but on weekends it occurs from 3 P.M. until 7 A.M.

13. Which person was wearing red sneakers?

    A. Black male
    B. Hispanic male
    C. Black female
    D. White male

14. Mrs. Gold stated the drugs were located

    A. under the blue van
    B. inside the black shoulder bag
    C. under the black car
    D. inside the brown paper bag

15. At what time does Mrs. Gold state the drugs are sold on weekends?

    A. 7:30 A.M. - 3:30 P.M.
    B. 7:00 A.M. - 1:00 P.M.
    C. 5:00 P.M. - 12:00 A.M.
    D. 3:00 P.M. - 7:00 A.M.

16. Police Communications Technician Bentley receives a call of an auto being stripped. He obtains the following information from the caller:
    Place of Occurrence: Corner of West End Avenue and W. 72nd Street
    Time of Occurrence: 10:30 P.M.
    Witness: Mr. Simpson
    Suspects: Two white males
    Crime: Auto stripping
    Action Taken: Suspects fled before police arrived

Communications Technician Bentley is about to enter the incident into the computer and send the information to the dispatcher.
Which one of the following expresses the above information MOST clearly and accurately?

- A. At 10:30 P.M., Mr. Simpson witnessed two white males stripping an auto parked at the corner of West End Avenue and W. 72nd Street. The suspects fled before the police arrived.
- B. An auto was parked at the corner of West End Avenue and W. 72nd Street. Two white males who were stripping at 10:30 P.M. were witnessed by Mr. Simpson. Before the police arrived, the suspects fled.
- C. Mr. Simpson saw two white males at the corner of West End Avenue and W. 72nd Street. Fleeing the scene before the police arrived, the witness saw the suspects strip an auto.
- D. Before the police arrived at 10:30 P.M. on the corner of West End Avenue and W. 72nd Street, Mr. Simpson witnessed two white males. The suspects, who stripped an auto, fled the scene.

17. 911 Operator Washington receives a call of a robbery and obtains the following information regarding the incident:

Place of Occurrence:	First National Bank, 45 West 96th Street
Time of Occurrence:	2:55 P.M.
Amount Taken:	$10,000
Description of Suspect:	Male, black, wearing a leather jacket, blue jeans, and white shirt
Weapon:	Gun

911 Operator Washington is about to enter the call into the computer.
Which one of the following expresses the above information MOST clearly and accurately?

- A. At 2:55 P.M., the First National Bank, located at 45 West 96th Street, was robbed at gunpoint of $10,000. The suspect is a black male and is wearing a leather jacket, blue jeans, and a white shirt.
- B. Ten thousand dollars was robbed from the First National Bank at 2:55 P.M. A black male was wearing a leather jacket, blue jeans, and a white shirt at 45 West 96th Street. He also had a gun.
- C. At 2:55 P.M., a male was wearing a leather jacket, blue jeans, and a white shirt. The First National Bank located at 45 West 96th Street was robbed by a black male. Ten thousand dollars was taken at gunpoint.
- D. Robbing the First National Bank, a male wore a leather jacket, blue jeans, and a white shirt at gunpoint. A black male was at 45 W. 96th Street. At 2:55 P.M., $10,000 was taken.

Questions 18-20.

DIRECTIONS: Questions 18 through 20 are to be answered SOLELY on the basis of the following passage.

Police Communications Technician Gordon receives a call from a male stating there is a bomb set to explode in the gym of Public School 85 in two hours. Realizing the urgency of the call, the Communications Technician calls the radio dispatcher, who assigns Patrol Car 43A to the scene. Communications Technician Gordon then notifies her supervisor, Miss Smith, who first reviews the tape of the call, then calls the Operations Unit which is notified of all serious incidents, and she reports the facts. The Operations Unit notifies the Mayor's Information Agency and Borough Headquarters of the emergency situation.

18. Who did Communications Technician Gordon notify FIRST?

    A. Supervisor Smith
    B. Operations Unit
    C. Patrol Car 43A
    D. Radio dispatcher

19. The Operations Unit was notified

    A. to inform school personnel of the bomb
    B. so they can arrive at the scene before the bomb is scheduled to go off
    C. to evacuate the school
    D. due to the seriousness of the incident

20. Who did Miss Smith notify?

    A. Patrol Car 43A
    B. Operations Unit
    C. Mayor's Information Agency
    D. Borough Headquarters

KEY (CORRECT ANSWERS)

1.	D	11.	C
2.	C	12.	B
3.	A	13.	D
4.	A	14.	B
5.	C	15.	D
6.	A	16.	A
7.	D	17.	A
8.	B	18.	D
9.	C	19.	D
10.	C	20.	B

TEST 2

DIRECTIONS: Each question or incomplete statement is followed by several suggested answers or completions. Select the one that BEST answers the question or completes the statement. *PRINT THE LETTER OF THE CORRECT ANSWER IN THE SPACE AT THE RIGHT.*

1. A Police Communications Technician receives a call reporting a large gathering. She obtained the following information:
   Place of Occurrence: Cooper Square Park
   Time of Occurrence: 1:15 A.M.
   Occurrence: Youths drinking and playing loud music
   Complainant: Mrs. Tucker, 20 Cooper Square
   Action Taken: Police scattered the crowd
   Communications Technician Carter is about to relay the information to the dispatcher.
   Which one of the following expresses the above information MOST clearly and accurately?

   A. The police responded to Cooper Square Park because Mrs. Tucker, who called 911, lives at 20 Cooper Square. The group of youths was scattered due to drinking and playing loud music at 1:15 A.M.
   B. Mrs. Tucker, who lives at 20 Cooper Square, called 911 to make a complaint of a group of youths who were drinking and playing loud music in Cooper Square Park at 1:15 A.M. The police responded and scattered the crowd.
   C. Loud music and drinking in Cooper Square Park by a group of youths caused the police to respond and scatter the crowd. Mrs. Tucker called 911 and complained. At 1:15 A.M., she lives at 20 Cooper Square.
   D. Playing loud music and drinking, Mrs. Tucker called the police. The police scattered a group of youths in Cooper Square Park at 1:15 A.M. Mrs. Tucker lives at 20 Cooper Square.

2. Dispatcher Weston received a call from the owner of a gas station and obtained the following information:
   Place of Occurrence: Blin's Gas Station, 1800 White Plains Road
   Time of Occurrence: 10:30 A.M.
   Occurrence: Left station without paying
   Witness: David Perilli
   Description of Auto: A white Firebird, license plate GEB275
   Suspect: Male, white, wearing blue jeans and a black T-shirt
   Dispatcher Weston is about to enter the information into the computer.
   Which one of the following expresses the above information MOST clearly and accurately?

   A. At 10:30 A.M., David Perilli witnessed a white male wearing blue jeans and a black T-shirt leave Blin's Gas Station, located at 1800 White Plains Road, without paying. The suspect was driving a white Firebird with license plate GEB275.
   B. Wearing blue jeans and a black T-shirt, David Perilli witnessed a white male leave Blin's Gas Station without paying. He was driving a white Firebird with license plate GEB275. This occurred at 1800 White Plains Road at 10:30 A.M.
   C. David Perilli witnessed a male wearing blue jeans and a black T-shirt driving a white Firebird. At 10:30 A.M., a white male left Blin's Gas Station, located at 1800 White Plains Road, without paying. His license plate was GEB275.

D. At 10:30 A.M., David Perilli witnessed a white male leaving Blin's Gas Station without paying. The driver of a white Firebird, license plate GEB275, was wearing blue jeans and a black T-shirt at 1800 White Plains Road.

Questions 3-4.

DIRECTIONS: Questions 3 and 4 are to be answered SOLELY on the basis of the following information.

Police Communications Technicians are required to assist callers who need non-emergency assistance. The callers are referred to non-emergency agencies. Listed below are some non-emergency situations and the agencies to which they should be referred.

Agency
Local Precinct — Unoccupied suspicious car
Environmental Protection Agency — Open fire hydrant
Sanitation Department — Abandoned car
S.P.C.A. — Injured, stray or sick animal
Transit Authority — Transit Authority travel information

3. Communications Technician Carter received a call from Mr. Cane, who stated that a car without license plates had been parked in front of his house for five days. Mr. Crane should be referred to the

   A. A.S.P.C.A.
   B. Transit Authority
   C. Sanitation Department
   D. Environmental Protection Agency

4. Mrs. Dunbar calls to report that a dog has been hit by a car and is lying at the curb in front of her house. Mrs. Dunbar should be referred to the

   A. Sanitation Department
   B. Local Precinct
   C. Environmental Protection Agency
   D. A.S.P.C.A.

5. Operator Bryant received a call of a robbery and obtained the following information:
   Place of Occurrence: Deluxe Deli, 303 E. 30th Street
   Time of Occurrence: 5:00 P.M.
   Crime: Robbery of $300
   Victim: Bonnie Smith, cashier of Deluxe Deli
   Description of Suspect: White, female, blonde hair, wearing black slacks and a red shirt
   Weapon: Knife

   Operator Bryant is about to enter this information into the computer.
   Which one of the following expresses the above information MOST clearly and accurately?

A. Bonnie Smith, the cashier of the Deluxe Deli reported at 5:00 P.M. that she was robbed of $300 at knifepoint at 303 East 30th Street. A white female with blonde hair was wearing black slacks and a red shirt.
B. At 5:00 P.M., a blonde-haired female robbed the 303 East 30th Street store. At the Deluxe Deli, cashier Bonnie Smith was robbed of $300 by a white female at knifepoint. She was wearing black slacks and a red shirt.
C. In a robbery that occurred at knifepoint, a blonde-haired white female robbed $300 from the Deluxe Deli. Bonnie Smith, cashier of the 303 East 30th Street store, said she was wearing black slacks and a red shirt at 5:00 P.M.
D. At 5:00 P.M., Bonnie Smith, cashier of the Deluxe Deli, located at 303 East 30th Street, was robbed of $300 at knifepoint. The suspect is a white female with blonde hair wearing black slacks and a red shirt.

6. 911 Operator Landers receives a call reporting a burglary that happened in the past. He obtained the following information from the caller:

Place of Occurrence: 196 Simpson Street
Date of Occurrence: June 12
Time of Occurrence: Between 8:30 A.M. and 7:45 P.M.
Victim: Mr. Arnold Frank
Items Stolen: $300 cash, stereo, assorted jewelry, and a VCR

911 Operator Landers is about to enter the incident into the computer.
Which one of the following expresses the above information MOST clearly and accurately?

A. Mr. Arnold Frank stated that on June 12, between 8:30 A.M. and 7:45 P.M., someone broke into his home at 196 Simpson Street and took $300 in cash, a stereo, assorted jewelry, and a VCR.
B. Mr. Arnold Frank stated between 8:30 A.M. and 7:45 P.M., he lives at 196 Simpson Street. A stereo, VCR, $300 in cash, and assorted jewelry were taken on June 12.
C. Between 8:30 A.M. and 7:45 P.M. on June 12, Mr. Arnold Frank reported someone broke into his home. At 196 Simpson Street, a VCR, $300 in cash, a stereo, and assorted jewelry were taken.
D. A stereo, VCR, $300 in cash, and assorted jewelry were taken between 8:30 M. and 7:45 P.M. On June 12, Mr. Arnold Frank reported he lives at 196 Simpson Street.

Questions 7-9.

DIRECTIONS: Questions 7 through 9 are to be answered SOLELY on the basis of the following passage.

Communications Operator Harris receives a call from Mrs. Stein who reports that a car accident occurred in front of her home. She states that one of the cars belongs to her neighbor, Mrs. Brown, and the other car belongs to Mrs. Stein's son, Joseph Stein. Communications Operator Harris enters Mrs. Stein's address into the computer and receives information that no such address exists. She asks Mrs. Stein to repeat her address. Mrs. Stein repeats her address and states that gasoline is leaking from the cars and that smoke is coming from their engines. She further states that people are trapped in the cars and then hangs up.

Communications Operator Harris notifies her supervisor, Jones, that she received a call but was unable to verify the address and that the caller hung up. Mrs. Jones listens to the tape of the call and finds that the caller stated 450 Park Place not 415 Park Place. She advises Communications Operator Harris to enter the correct address, then notify Emergency Service Unit to respond to the individuals trapped in the cars, the Fire Department for the smoke condition, and Emergency Medical Service for any possible injuries.

7. Who did Communications Operator Harris notify concerning the problem with the caller's address?   7._____

    A. Mrs. Brown   B. Joseph Stein
    C. Joseph Brown   D. Mrs. Jones

8. Which agency was Communications Operator Harris advised to notify concerning individuals trapped in the cars?   8._____

    A. Emergency Medical Service
    B. Fire Department
    C. Emergency Service Unit
    D. NYC Police Department

9. Which agency did Supervisor Jones advise Communications Operator Harris to notify for the smoke condition?   9._____

    A. NYC Police Department
    B. Emergency Medical Service
    C. Fire Department
    D. Emergency Service Unit

Question 10.

DIRECTIONS: Question 10 is to be answered SOLELY on the basis of the following information.

When a Police Communications Technician receives a call concerning a bank robbery, a Communications Technician should do the following in the order given:

    I. Get address and name of the bank from the caller.
    II. Enter the address into the computer.
    III. Use the *Hotline* button to alert the dispatcher of the serious incident going into the computer.
    IV. Get back to the caller and get the description of the suspect and other pertinent information.
    V. Enter additional information into the computer and send it to the dispatcher.
    VI. Upgrade the seriousness of the incident so it appears first on dispatcher's screen.
    VII. Notify the Supervising Police Communications Technician of the bank robbery.

10. Police Communications Technician Brent receives a call from Mr. Ross stating that while he was on line at the Trust Bank, at West 34th Street and 9th Avenue, he witnessed a bank robbery. Communications Technician Brent enters the address into the computer, then presses the *Hotline* button and alerts the dispatcher that there was a bank robbery at the Trust Bank on West 34th Street and 9th Avenue. Mr. Ross continues to state that the robber is a white male in his 30's wearing a light blue shirt and blue jeans.
After obtaining other pertinent information, the NEXT step Communications Technician Brent should take is to

    A. enter additional information into the computer and send it to the dispatcher
    B. upgrade the seriousness of the incident so it appears first on the dispatcher's screen
    C. notify his supervisor of the bank robbery
    D. use the *Hotline* button to alert the dispatcher of a serious incident going into the computer

11. Dispatcher Wilson receives a call regarding drugs being sold in the lobby of an apartment building. He obtains the following information:
    Place of Occurrence: 305 Willis Avenue
    Time of Occurrence: 2:00 P.M.
    Witnesses: Roy Rodriguez and Harry Armstrong
    Suspect: Melvin Talbot, left the scene before the police arrived
    Crime: Drug sale
    Dispatcher Wilson is about to enter this incident into the computer.
    Which one of the following expresses the above information MOST clearly and accurately?

    A. Roy Rodriguez and Harry Armstrong reported that they witnessed Melvin Talbot selling drugs in the lobby of 305 Willis Avenue at 2:00 P.M. The suspect left the scene before the police arrived.
    B. In the lobby, Roy Rodriguez reported at 2:00 P.M. he saw Melvin Talbot selling drugs with Harry Armstrong. He left the lobby of 305 Willis Avenue before the police arrived.
    C. Roy Rodriguez and Harry Armstrong witnessed drugs being sold at 305 Willis Avenue. Before the police arrived at 2:00 P.M., Melvin Talbot left the lobby.
    D. Before the police arrived, witnesses stated that Melvin Talbot was selling drugs. At 305 Willis Avenue, in the lobby, Roy Rodriguez and Harry Armstrong said he left the scene at 2:00 P.M.

12. Operator Rogers receives a call of a car being stolen. He obtains the following information:
    Place of Occurrence: Parking lot at 1723 East 20th Street
    Time of Occurrence: 2:30 A.M.
    Vehicle Involved: 1988 Toyota Corolla
    Suspects: Male, Hispanic, wearing a red T-shirt
    Crime: Auto theft
    Witness: Janet Alonzo
    Operator Rogers is entering the information into the computer.
    Which one of the following expresses the above information MOST clearly and accurately?

A. At 2:30 A.M., wearing a red T-shirt, Janet Alonzo witnessed a 1988 Toyota Corolla being stolen by a male Hispanic in the parking lot at 1723 East 20th Street.
B. A male Hispanic, wearing a red T-shirt, was in the parking lot at 1723 East 20th Street." At 2:30 A.M., Janet Alonzo witnessed a 1988 Toyota Corolla being stolen.
C. At 2:30 A.M., Janet Alonzo witnessed a 1988 Toyota Corolla in the parking lot at 1723 East 20th Street being stolen by a male Hispanic who is wearing a red T-shirt.
D. Janet Alonzo witnessed a 1988 Toyota Corolla in the parking lot being stolen. At 2:30 A.M., a male Hispanic was wearing a red T-shirt at 1723 East 20th Street.

Question 13.

DIRECTIONS: Question 13 is to be answered SOLELY on the basis of the following information.

There are times when Police Communications Technicians have to reassign officers in a patrol car from a less serious incident which does not require immediate police response to an incident of a more serious nature which does require immediate police response. Police Communications Technicians must choose among the assigned patrol cars and determine which one is assigned to the least serious incident, then reassign that one to the situation which requires immediate police response.

Communications Technician Reese is working the 13th Division which covers the 79th Precinct. There are only four patrol cars working in the 79th Precinct. They are assigned as follows:

79A is assigned to a car accident with injuries involving an intoxicated driver.

79B is assigned to a group of teenagers playing loud music in a park.

79C is assigned to a group of teenagers trying to steal liquor in a liquor store, who are possibly armed with guns.

79D is assigned to a suspicious man in a bank, with possible intentions to rob the bank.

13. If Communications Technician Reese receives a call of an incident that requires immediate police response, which patrol car should be reassigned?

A. 79A B. 79B C. 79C D. 79D

Questions 14-16.

DIRECTIONS: Questions 14 through 16 are to be answered SOLELY on the basis of the following information.

On May 12, at 3:35 P.M., Police Communications Technician Connor receives a call from a child caller requesting an ambulance for her mother, whom she cannot wake. The child did not know her address, but gave Communications Technician Connor her apartment number and telephone number. Communications Technician Connor's supervisor, Ms. Bendel, is advised of the situation and consult's Cole's Directory, a listing published by the Bell Telephone Company, to obtain an address when only the telephone number is known. The telephone number is unlisted. Ms. Bendel asks Communications Technician Taylor to call Telco Security to obtain an address from their telephone number listing. Communications Technician Taylor speaks to Ms. Morris of Telco Security and obtains the address. Communications Technician Connor, who is still talking with the child, is given the address by Communications Technician Taylor. She enters the information into the computer system and transfers the caller to the Emergency Medical Service.

14. What information did Communications Technician Connor obtain from the child caller?   14.____

    A. Telephone number and apartment number
    B. Name and address
    C. Address and telephone number
    D. Apartment number and address

15. Communications Technician Taylor obtained the address from   15.____

    A. Communications Technician Connor
    B. Ms. Morris
    C. Supervisor Bendel
    D. the child caller

16. The caller's address was obtained by calling   16.____

    A. Cole's Directory
    B. Telco Security
    C. Emergency Medical Service
    D. The Telephone Company

Question 17.

DIRECTIONS: Question 17 is to be answered SOLELY on the basis of the following information.

The following incidents appear on the Police Communications Technician's computer screen which were called in by three different callers at the same time:
  I. At 3040 Hill Avenue between Worth and Centre Streets, there are two people fighting in the third floor hallway. One of them has a shiny metal object.
  II. In a building located on Hill Avenue between Worth and Centre Streets, a man and a woman are having an argument on the third floor. The woman has a knife in her hand.
  III. In front of Apartment 3C on the third floor, a husband and wife are yelling at each other. The wife is pointing a metal letter opener at her husband. The building is located on the corner of Hill Avenue and Worth Street.

17. A Police Communications Technician may be required to combine into one incident many calls that appear on the computer screen if they seem to be reporting the same incident. Which of the above should a Police Communications Technician combine into one incident?   17.____

    A. I and II   B. I and III
    C. II and III   D. I, II, and III

Questions 18-19.

DIRECTIONS: Questions 18 and 19 are to be answered SOLELY on the basis of the following information.

Police Communications Technicians must be able to identify and assign codes to the crimes described in the calls they receive. All crimes are coded by number and by priority. The priority code number indicates the seriousness of the crime. The lower the priority number, the more serious the crime.

Listed below is a chart of several crimes and their definitions. The corresponding crime code and priority code number are given.

CRIME	DEFINITION	CRIME CODE	PRIORITY CODE
Criminal Mischief:	Occurs when a person intentionally damages another person's property	29	6
Harrassment:	Occurs when a person intentionally annoys another person by striking, shoving, or kicking them without causing injury	27	8
Aggravated Harrassment:	Occurs when a person intentionally annoys another person by using any form of communication	28	9
Theft of Service:	Occurs when a person intentionally avoids payment for services given	25	7

18. Communications Technician Rogers received a call from Mrs. Freeman, who stated that her next door neighbor, whom she had an argument with, has thrown a rock through her apartment window.
    Which one of the following is the CORRECT crime code?

    A. 29   B. 28   C. 27   D. 25

19. Communications Technician Tucker received a call from a man who stated that he is a waiter at the Frontier Diner. He states that one of his customers was refusing to pay for his meal.
    Which one of the following is the CORRECT priority code number for this crime?

    A. 6   B. 7   C. 8   D. 9

    Dispatcher Matthews received a call of a bomb threat. He obtained the following information;
    Address of Occurrence: 202 Church Avenue
    Location: 2nd floor men's room
    Time of Call: 12:00 P.M.
    Time of Occurrence: 2:00 P.M.
    Terrorist Organization: People *Against Government*

Caller: Anonymous male member of *People* Against Government
Action Taken: Supervisor Jones notified of the bomb threat

Dispatcher Matthews is about to enter the information into the computer.
Which one of the following expresses the above information MOST clearly and accurately?

A. An anonymous male called Dispatcher Matthews and told him that a bomb is set to go off at 202 Church Avenue in the 2nd floor men's room at 2:00 P.M. Dispatcher Matthews notified Supervisor Jones that the caller is from *People Against Government* at 12:00 P.M.
B. Dispatcher Matthews received a call in the 2nd floor men's room of a bomb threat from an anonymous male member of the *People Against Government* terrorist organization. He notified Supervisor Jones at 12:00 P.M. that a bomb is set to go off at 2:00 P.M. at 202 Church Avenue.
C. Dispatcher Matthews received a call at 202 Church Avenue from the *People Against Government,* a terrorist organization. An anonymous male stated that a bomb is set to go off at 2:00 P.M. in the 2nd floor men's room. At 12:00 P.M., Dispatcher Matthews notified Supervisor Jones of the call.
D. At 12:00 P.M., Dispatcher Matthews received a call from an anonymous male caller who states that he is from a terrorist organization known as *People Against Government.* He states that a bomb has been placed in the 2nd floor men's room of 202 Church Avenue and is set to go off at 2:00 P.M. Dispatcher Matthews notified Supervisor Jones of the bomb threat.

KEY (CORRECT ANSWERS)

1.	B	11.	A
2.	A	12.	C
3.	C	13.	B
4.	D	14.	A
5.	D	15.	B
6.	A	16.	B
7.	D	17.	D
8.	C	18.	A
9.	C	19.	B
10.	A	20.	D

EXAMINATION SECTION
TEST 1

DIRECTIONS: Each question or incomplete statement is followed by several suggested answers or completions. Select the one that BEST answers the question or completes the statement. *PRINT THE LETTER OF THE CORRECT ANSWER IN THE SPACE AT THE RIGHT.*

1. You answer a phone complaint from a person concerning an improper labeling practice in a shop in his neighborhood. Upon listening to the complaint, you get the impression that the person is exaggerating and may be too excited to view the matter clearly.
   Of the following, your BEST course would be to
   A. tell the man that you can understand his anger but think it is not a really serious problem
   B. suggest to the man that he file a complaint with the Department of Consumer Affairs
   C. tell the man to stay away from the shop and have his friends do the same
   D. take down the information that the man offers so that he will see that the Police Department is concerned

   1.____

2. Suppose that late at night you receive a call on 911. The caller turns out to be an elderly man who is not able to get out much and who is calling you not because he needs help but because he wants to talk with someone.
   The BEST way to handle such a situation is to
   A. explain to him that the number is for emergencies and his call may prevent others from getting the help they need
   B. talk to him if not many calls are coming in but excuse yourself and cut him off if you are busy
   C. cut him off immediately when you find out he does not need help because this will be the most effective way of discouraging him
   D. suggest that he call train or bus information as the clerks there are often not busy at night

   2.____

3. While you are on duty, you receive a call from a person whose name your recognize to be that of a person who calls frequently about matters of no importance. The caller requests your name and your supervisor's name so that she can report you for being impolite to her.
   You should
   A. ask her when and how you were impolite to her
   B. tell her that she should not call about such minor matters
   C. make a report about her complaint for your superior
   D. give her the information that she requests

   3.____

33

4. Of the following, the MOST important reason for requiring each employ of the Police Department to be responsible for good public relations is that
   A. the Police Department has better morale when employees join in an effort to improve public relations
   B. the public judges the Department according to impressions received at every level in the Department
   C. most employees will not behave well toward the public unless required to do so
   D. employees who improve public relations will receive commendations from superiors

5. Assume that you are in the Bureau of Public Relations. You receive a telephone call from a citizen who asks if a study has been made of the advisability of combining the city's police and fire departments. Assume that you have no information on the subject.
   Of the following, your BEST course would be to
   A. tell the caller that undoubtedly the subject has been studied but that you do not have the information available
   B. suggest to the caller that he telephone the Fire Department's Community Relations section for further information
   C. explain to the caller that the functions of the two departments are distinct and that combining them would be inefficient
   D. take the caller's number in order to call back, and then find information or referrals to give him

6. Suppose that Police Department officials have discouraged representatives of the press from contacting police administrative aides (except aides in the Public Relations Bureau) for information.
   Of the following, the BEST reason for such a policy would be to
   A. assure proper control over information released to the press by the Department
   B. increase the value of official press releases of the Department
   C. make press representatives realize that the Department is not seeking publicity
   D. reduce the chance of crimes being committed in imitation of those reported in the press

7. People who phone the Police Department often use excited, emotional, and sometimes angry speech.
   The BEST policy for you to take when speaking to this type of caller is to
   A. tell the person directly that he must speak in a more civil way
   B. tell the caller to call back when he is in a better mood
   C. give the person time to settle down, by doing most of the talking yourself
   D. speak calmly yourself to help the caller to gradually become more relaxed

8. On a particularly busy evening, the police administrative aide assigned to the telephones had answered a tremendous number of inquiries and complaints by irate citizens. His patience was exhausted when he received a call from a citizen who reported, *Officer, a bird just flew into my bedroom. What should I do?* In a release of tension, the aide responded, *Keep it for seven days; and if no one claims it, it is yours.*
This response by the aide would usually be considered
   A. *advisable*, because the person should see how unusual his question was
   B. *advisable*, because he avoided offering police services that were unavailable
   C. *not advisable*, because such a remark might be regarded as insulting rather than humorous
   D. *not advisable*, because the person might not want a bird for a pet

9. While temporarily assigned to switchboard duty, you receive a call from a man who says his uncle in Pittsburgh has just called him and threatened to commit suicide. The man is convinced his uncle intends to carry out his threat.
Of the following, you should
   A. advise the man to have neighbors of the uncle check to see if the uncle is all right
   B. politely inform the man that such out-of-town incidents are beyond the authority of the local precinct
   C. take the uncle's name, address, and telephone number and immediately contact police authorities in Pittsburgh
   D. get the man's name, address, and telephone number so that you can determine whether the call is a hoax

10. Assume that in the course of your assigned duties you have just taken a necessary action which you feel has angered a citizen. After he has gone, you suddenly realize that the incident might result in an unjustified complaint.
The MOST advisable action for you to take now would be to
   A. contact the person and apologize to him
   B. make complete notes on the incident and on any witnesses who might be helpful
   C. ask your superior what you might expect in case of such a complaint, without giving any hint of the actual occurrence
   D. accept the situation as one of the hazards of your job

11. Your job may bring you in contact with people from the community who are confronted with emergencies,, and are experiencing feelings of tension, anxiety, or even hostility. It is good to keep in mind what attitude is most helpful to people who, in such situations like these.
Which of the following would be BEST to do?
   A. Present similar examples of your own problems to make the person feel that his problems are not unusual.
   B. Recognize the person's feelings, present information on available services, and make suggestions as to proper procedures

C. Expect that some of the information is exaggerated and encourage the person to let some time pass before seeking further help.
D. Have the person wait while you try to make arrangements for his problem to be solved.

12. Suppose that while on duty you receive a call from the owner of a gas station which is located within the precinct. The owner is annoyed with a certain rule made by the Police Department which concerns the operation of such stations. You agree with him.
Of the following, the BEST action for you to take is to
    A. make a report on the call and suggest to the owner that he write a letter to the Department about the rule
    B. tell the owner that there is little that can be done since such rules are departmental policy
    C. tell the owner that you agree with his complaint and that you will write a memo of his call
    D. establish good relations with the owner by suggesting how to word a letter that will get action from the department

12.____

13. Suppose that you are working at the switchboard when a call comes in late at night from a woman who reports that her neighbors are having a very noisy party. She gives you her first name, surname, and address, and you ask her title is *Miss* or *Mrs*. She replies that her title is irrelevant to her complaint, and wants to know why you ask.
Of the following possible ways of handling this, which is BEST?
    A. Insist that the title is necessary for identification purposes
    B. Tell her that it is merely to find out what her marital status is
    C. Agree that the information is not necessary and ask her how she wants to be referred to
    D. Find out why she shows such a peculiar reaction to a request for harmless information

13.____

14. While covering an assignment on the switchboard, you receive a call from a young girl who tells you of rumored plans for a gang fight in her neighborhood. You should
    A. take down the information so that a patrol squad can investigate the area and possibly keep the fight from starting
    B. discourage the girl from becoming alarmed by reminding her that it is only a rumor
    C. realize that this is a teenager looking for attention, humor her, and dismiss the matter
    D. take down the information but tell the girl that you need concrete information, and not just rumors, to take any action on her call

14.____

15. The one of the following which would MOST likely lead to friction among police administrative aides in a unit would be for the supervisor in charge of the unit to
    A. defend the actions of the aides he supervises when discussing them with his own supervisor

15.____

B. get his men to work together as a team in completing the work of the unit
C. praise each of the aides he supervises *in confidence* as the best aide in the unit
D. consider the point of view of the aides he supervises when assigning unpleasant tasks

16. Suppose that a police administrative aide who had been transferred to your office from another unit in your Department because of difficulties with his supervisor has been placed under your supervision.
   The BEST course of action for you to take FIRST is to
   A. analyze the aide's past grievance to determine if the transfer was the best settlement of the problem
   B. advise him of the difficulties his former supervisor had with other employees and encourage him not to feel bad about the transfer
   C. warn him that you will not tolerate any nonsense and that he will be watched carefully while assigned to your unit
   D. instruct him in the duties he will be performing in your unit and make him feel *wanted* in his new position

17. In which of the following circumstances would it be MOST appropriate for you to use an impersonal style of writing rather than a personal style, which relies on the use of personal pronouns and other personal references?
   When writing a memorandum to
   A. give your opinion to an associate on the advisability of holding a weekly staff meeting
   B. furnish your superior with data justifying a proposed outlay of funds for new equipment
   C. give your version of an incident which resulted in a complaint by a citizen about your behavior
   D. support your request for a transfer to another division

18. A newly appointed supervisor should learn as much as possible about the backgrounds of his subordinates.
   The statement is generally CORRECT because
   A. effective handling of subordinates is based upon knowledge of their individual differences
   B. knowing their backgrounds assures they will be treated objectively, equally, and without favor
   C. some subordinates perform more efficiently under one supervisor than under another
   D. subordinates have confidence in a supervisor who knows all about them

19. You have found it necessary, for valid reasons, to criticize the work of one of the female police administrative aides. She later comes to your desk and accuses you of criticizing her work because she is a woman.
   The BEST way for you to deal with this employee is to
   A. ask her to apologize, since you would never allow yourself to be guilty of his kind of discrimination

B. discuss her complaint with her, explaining again and at greater length the reason for your criticism
C. assure her you wish to be fair, and ask her to submit a written report to you on her complaint
D. apologize for hurting her feelings and promise that she will be left alone in the future

20. The following steps are recognized steps in teaching an employee a new skill:
    I. Demonstrate how to do the work
    II. Let the learner do the work himself
    III. Explain the nature and purpose of the work
    IV. Correct poor procedures by suggestion and demonstration
    The CORRECT order for these steps is
    A. III, II, IV, I   B. II, I, III, IV   C. III, I, II, IV   D. I, III, II, IV

21. Suppose you have arranged an interview with a subordinate to try to help him overcome a serious shortcoming in his technical work. While you do not intend to talk to him about his attitude, you have noticed that he seems to be suspicious and resentful of people in authority. You need a record of the points covered in the discussion since further interviews are likely to be necessary.
    Your BEST course would be to
    A. write a checklist of points you wish to discuss and carefully check the points off as the interview progresses
    B. know exactly how you wish to proceed, and then make written notes during the interview of your subordinate's comments
    C. frankly tell your subordinate that you are recording the talk on tape but place the recorder where it will not hinder discussion
    D. keep in mind what you wish to accomplish and make notes on the interview immediately after it is over

22. A police administrative aide has explained a complicated procedure to several subordinates. He has been talking clearly, allowing time for information to sink in. He has also encouraged questions. Yet, he still questions his subordinates after his explanation, with the obvious objective of finding out whether they completely understand the procedure.
    Under these circumstances, the action of the police administrative aide, in asking questions about the procedure, is
    A. *not advisable*, because subordinates who do not now know the procedure which has been explained so carefully can read and study it
    B. *not advisable*, because he endangers his relationship with his subordinates by insulting their intelligence
    C. *advisable*, because subordinate basically resent instructions and seldom give their full attention in a group situation
    D. *advisable*, because the answers to his questions help him to determine whether he has gained his objective

23. The most competent of the police administrative aides is a pleasant, intelligent young woman who breaks the rules of the Department by occasionally making long personal telephone calls during working hours. You have not talked to her up until now about this fault. However, the calls are beginning to increase, and you decide to deal directly with the problem.
The BEST way to approach the subject with her would be to
   A. review with her the history of her infractions of the rules
   B. point out that her conduct is not fair to the other workers
   C. tell her that her personal calls are excessive and discuss it with her
   D. warn her quietly that you intend to apply penalties if necessary

24. Assume that you are supervising eight male police administrative aides who do similar clerical work. A group of four of them work on each side of a row of files which can be moved without much trouble. You notice that in each group there is a clique of three aides, leaving one member isolated. The two isolated members are relative newcomers.
Your BEST course in such a case would be to
   A. ignore the situation because to concern yourself with informal social arrangements of your subordinates would distract you from more important matters
   B. ask each of the cliques to invite the isolated member in their working group to lunch with them from time to time
   C. tell each group that you cannot allow cliques to form as it is bad for the morale of the unit
   D. find an excuse to move the file cabinet to the side of the room and then move the desks of the two isolated members close together

25. Suppose that your supervisor, who has recently been promoted and transferred to your division, asks you to review a certain procedure with a view to its possible revision. You know that several years ago a sergeant made a lengthy and intensive report based on a similar review.
Which of the following would it be BEST for you to do FIRST?
   A. Ask your supervisor if he is aware of the previous report
   B. Read the sergeant's report before you begin work to see what bearing it has on your assignment
   C. Begin work on the review without reading his report so that you will have a fresh point of view
   D. Ask the sergeant to assist you in your review

26. Using form letters in business correspondence is LEAST effective when
   A. answering letters on a frequently recurring subject
   B. giving the same information to many addresses
   C. the recipient is only interested in the routing information contained in the form letter
   D. a reply must be keyed to the individual requirements of the intended reader

27. From the viewpoint of an office administrator, the BEST of the following reasons for distributing the incoming mail before the beginning of the regular work day is that
   A. distribution can be handled quickly and most efficiently at that time
   B. distribution later in the day may be distracting to or interfering with other employees
   C. the employees who distribute the mail can then perform other tasks during the rest of the day
   D. office activities for the day based on the mail may then be started promptly

28. Suppose you have had difficulty locating a document in the files because you could not decide where it should have been filed. You learn that other people in the office have had the same problem. You know that the document will be needed from time to time in the future.
   Your BEST course, when refiling the document, would be to
   A. make a written note of where you found it so that you will find it more easily the next time
   B. reclassify it and file it in the file where you first looked for it
   C. file it where you found it and put cross-reference sheets in the other likely files
   D. make a mental association to help you find it the next time and put it back where you found it

29. Suppose that your supervisor is attending a series of meetings of police captains in Philadelphia and will not be back until next Wednesday. He has left no instructions with you as to how you should handle telephone calls for him.
   In most instances, your BEST course of action would be to say:
   A. He isn't here just now.
   B. He is out of town and won't be back until next Wednesday.
   C. He won't be in today.
   D. He is in Philadelphia attending a meeting of police captains.

30. The one of the following which is USUALLY an important by-product of the preparation of a procedure manual is that
   A. information uncovered in the process of preparation may lead to improvement of procedures
   B. workers refer to the manual instead of bothering their supervisors for information
   C. supervisors use the manual for training stenographers
   D. employees have equal access to information needed to do their jobs

31. You have been asked to organize a clerical job and supervise police administrative aides who will do the actual work. The job consists of removing, from several boxes of data processing cards which are arranged in alphabetical order, the cards of those whose names appear on certain lists. The person removing the card then notes a date on the card. Assume that the work will be done accurately whatever system is used.

Which of the following statements describes both the MOST efficient method and the BEST reasons for using that method? Have
- A. two aides work together, one calling names and the other extracting cards, and dating them, because the average production of any two aides working together should be higher, under these circumstances, than that of any two aides working alone
- B. each aide work alone, because it is easier to check spelling when reading the names than when listening to them
- C. two aides work together, one calling names and the other extracting cards and dating them, because social interaction tends to make work go faster
- D. each aide work alone, because the average production of any two aides, each working alone, should be higher, under these circumstances, than that of any two aides working together

32. The term *work flow*, when used in connection with office management or the activities in an office GENERALLY means the 32._____
- A. rate of speed at which work flows through a single section of an office
- B. use of charts in the analysis of various office functions
- C. number of individual work units which can be produced by the average employee
- D. step-by-step physical routing of work through its various procedures

Questions 33-40.

DIRECTIONS:
Name of Offense   V A N D S B R U G H
Code Letter   c o m p l e x i t y
File Number   1 2 3 4 5 6 7 8 9 0

Assume that each of the above capital letters is the first letter of the name of an offense, that the small letter directly beneath each capita letter is the code letter for the offense, and that the number directly beneath each code letter is the file number for the offense.

In each of Questions 33 through 40, the code letters and file numbers should correspond to the capital letters.
If there is an error only in Column 2, mark your answer A.
If there is an error only in Column 3, mark your answer B.
If there is an error in both Column 2 and Column, mark your answer C.
If both Columns 2 and 3 are correct, mark your answer D.

Sample Questions:

COLUMN 1	COLUMN 2	COLUMN 3
BNARGHSVVU	emoxtylcci	6357905118

The code letters in Column 2 are correct, but the first 5 in Column 3 should be 2. Therefore, the answer is B.

	COLUMN 1	COLUMN 2	COLUMN 3	
33.	HGDSBNBSVR	ytplxmelcx	0945736517	33._____

34.	SDGUUNHVAH	lptiimycoy	5498830120	34.____
35.	BRSNAAVUDU	exlmooctpi	6753221848	35.____
36.	VSRUDNADUS	cleipmopil	1568432485	36.____
37.	NDSHVRBUAG	mplycxeiot	3450175829	37.____
38.	GHUSNVBRDA	tyilmcexpo	9805316742	38.____
39.	DBSHVURANG	pesycixomt	4650187239	39.____
40.	RHNNASBDGU	xymnolepti	7033256398	40.____

KEY (CORRECT ANSWERS)

1.	B	11.	B	21.	D	31.	D
2.	A	12.	A	22.	D	32.	D
3.	D	13.	C	23.	C	33.	C
4.	B	14.	A	24.	D	34.	D
5.	D	15.	C	25.	A	35.	A
6.	A	16.	D	26.	D	36.	C
7.	D	17.	B	27.	D	37.	B
8.	C	18.	A	28.	C	38.	D
9.	C	19.	B	29.	B	39.	A
10.	B	20.	C	30.	A	40.	C

SCANNING MAPS

One section of the exam tests your ability to orient yourself within a given region on a map. Using the map accompanying questions 1 through 3; choose the best way of getting from one point to another.

The New Bridge is closed to traffic because it has a broken span.

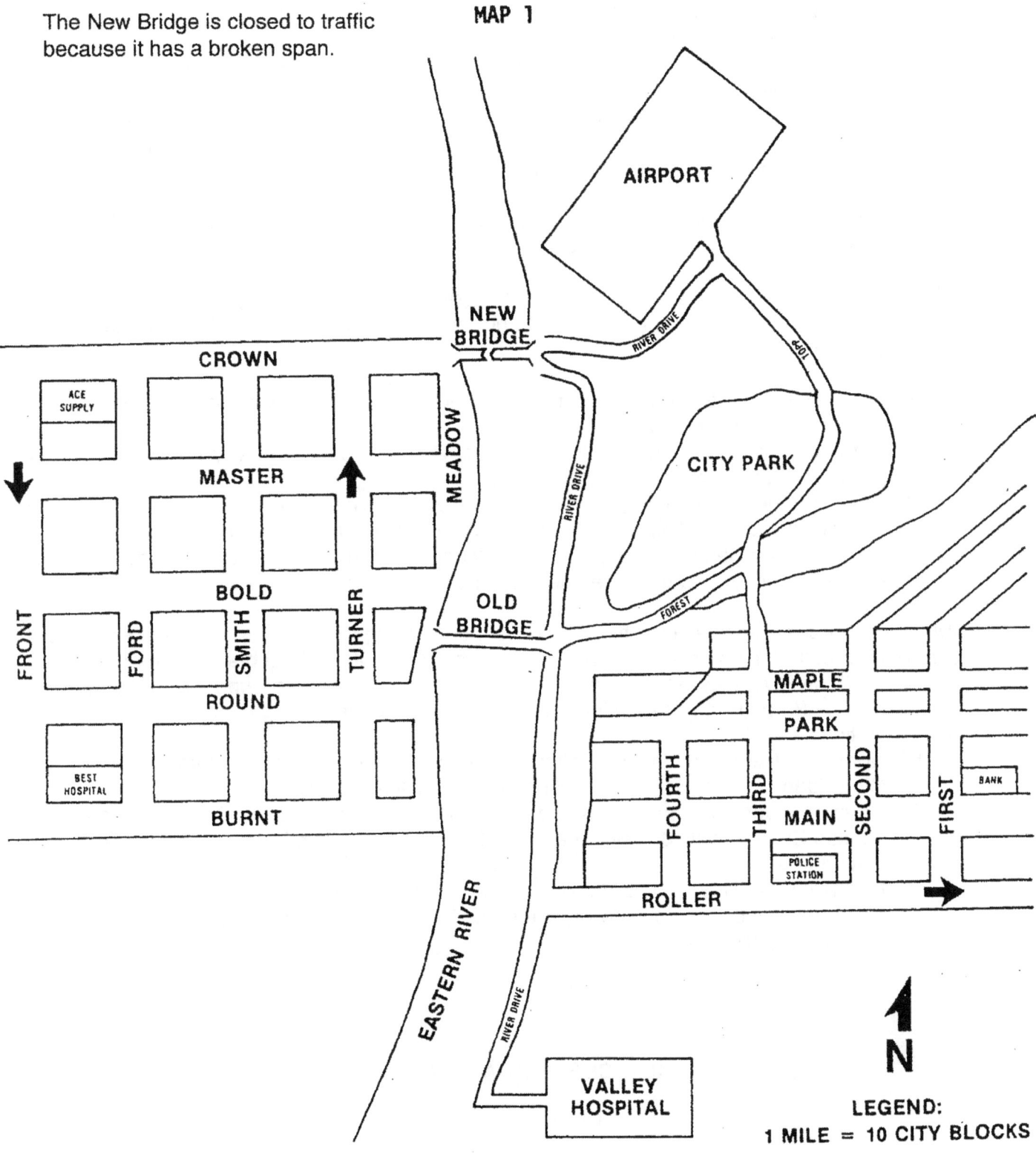

MAP 1

Arrows (———▶) indicate on-way traffic and direction of traffic. A street marked by an arrow is one way for the entire length of the street.

43

SAMPLE QUESTIONS

1. Officers in a patrol car which is at the Airport receive a call for assistance at Best Hospital. The shortest route without breaking the law is:
    A. Southwest on River Drive, right on Forest, cross Old Bridge, south on Meadow, and west on Burnt to hospital entrance.
    B. Southwest on River Drive, right on New Bridge, left on Meadow, west on Burnt to hospital entrance.
    C. Southwest on River Drive, right on Old Bridge, left on Turner, right on Burnt to hospital entrance.
    D. North on River Drive to Topp, through City Park to Forest, cross Old Bridge, left on Meadow, west on Burnt to hospital entrance.

2. After returning to the police station, the officers receive a call to pick up injured persons at an accident site (located on the east side of New Bridge) and return to Valley Hospital. The shortest route without breaking the law is:

    A. West on Roller, north on River Drive, left to accident scene at New Bridge, then north on River Drive to hospital entrance.
    B. North on Third, left on Forest, north on River Drive, left to accident scene at new Bridge, then south on River Drive to hospital entrance.
    C. East on Roller, left on First, west on Maple, north on Third, left on Forest, north on River Drive to accident scene at New Bridge, then south on River Drive to hospital entrance.
    D. North on Third, left on Forest, cross Old Bridge, north on Meadow to New Bridge, south on Meadow, east over Old Bridge, then south on River Drive to hospital entrance.

3. While at the Valley Hospital, the officers receive a call asking them to pick up materials at the Ace Supply and return them to the police station. The shortest route without breaking the law is:
    A. North on River Drive, cross New Bridge, west on Crown to Ace Supply, then south on Front, east on Burnt, north on Meadow, cross Old Bridge, east on Forest, south on Third to police station.
    B. North on River Drive, right on Roller to police station, then north on Third, left on Forest, cross Old Bridge, north on Meadow, west on Crown to Ace Supply.
    C. North on River Drive, cross Old Bridge, north on Meadow, west on Crown to Ace Supply, then east on Crown, south on Meadow, cross Old Bridge, east on Forest, south on Third to police station.
    D. North on River Drive, cross Old Bridge, south on Meadow, west on Burnt, north on Front to Ace Supply, then east on Crown, south on Meadow, cross Old Bridge, east on Forest, south on Third to police station.

KEY (CORRECT ANSWERS)

1. A
2. B
3. C

MAP READING

EXAMINATION SECTION
TEST 1

DIRECTIONS: Each question or incomplete statement is followed by several suggested answers or completions. Select the one that BEST answers the question or completes the statement. *PRINT THE LETTER OF THE CORRECT ANSWER IN THE SPACE AT THE RIGHT.*

Questions 1-3.

DIRECTIONS: Questions 1 through 3 are to be answered SOLELY on the basis of the map which appears on the next page. The flow of traffic is indicated by the arrow. If there is only one arrow shown, then traffic flows only in the direction indicated by the arrow. If there are two arrows shown, then traffic flows in both directions. You must follow the flow of traffic.

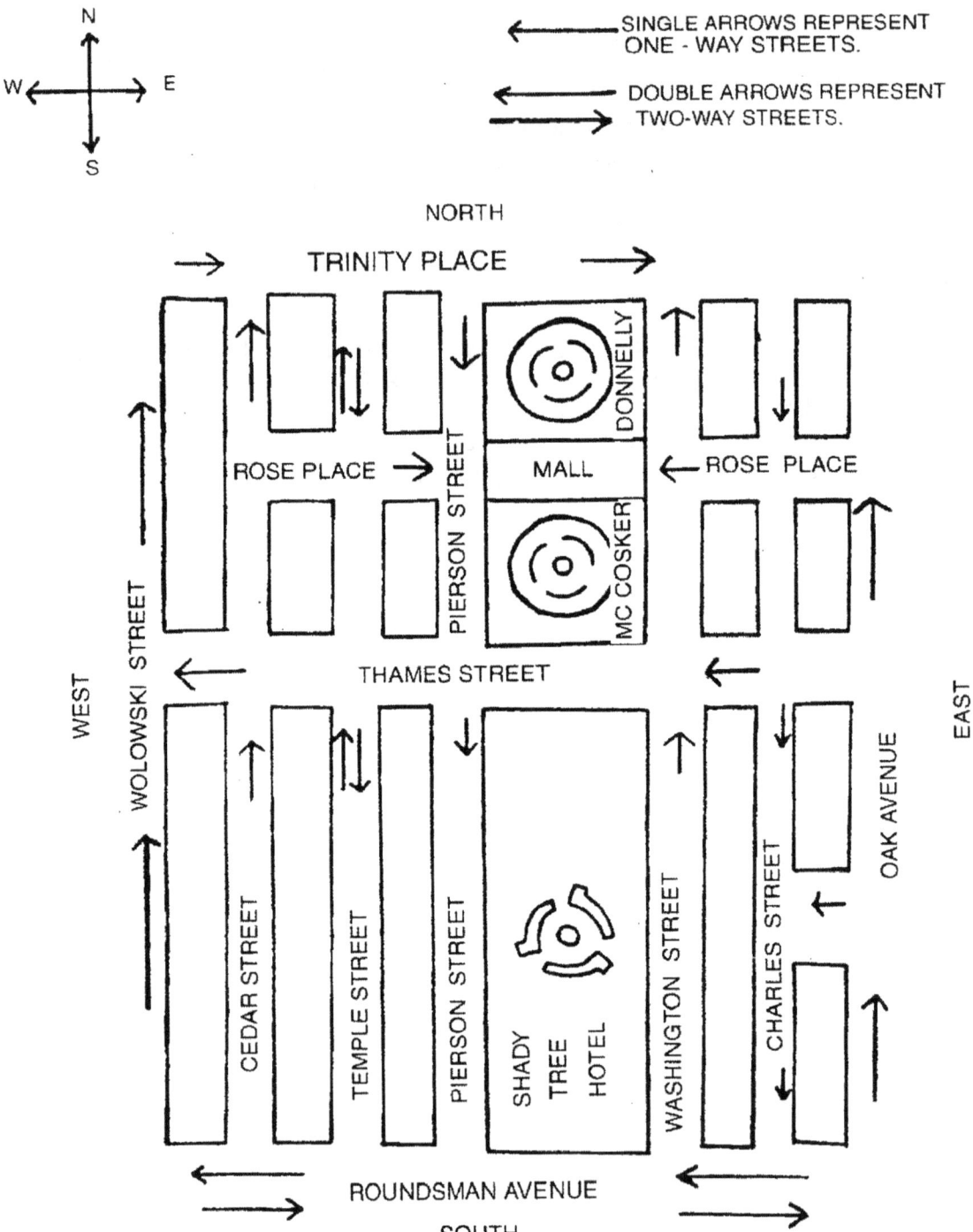

1. Police Officers Simms and O'Brien are located at Roundsman Avenue and Washington Street. The radio dispatcher has assigned them to investigate a motor vehicle accident at the corner of Pierson Street and Rose Place.
   Which one of the following is the SHORTEST route for them to take in their patrol car, making sure to obey all traffic regulations?
   Travel

   A. west on Roundsman Avenue, then north on Temple Street, then east on Thames Street, then north on Pierson Street to Rose Place
   B. east on Roundsman Avenue, then north on Oak Avenue, then west on Rose Place to Pierson Street
   C. west on Roundsman Avenue, then north on Temple Street, then east on Rose Place to Pierson Street
   D. east on Roundsman Avenue, then north on Oak Avenue, then west on Thames Street, then north on Temple Street, then east on Rose Place to Pierson Street

2. Police Officers Sears and Castro are located at Cedar Street and Roundsman Avenue. They are called to respond to the scene of a burglary at Rose Place and Charles Street.
   Which one of the following is the SHORTEST route for them to take in their patrol car, making sure to obey all traffic regulations?
   Travel

   A. east on Roundsman Avenue, then north on Oak Avenue, then west on Rose Place to Charles Street
   B. east on Roundsman Avenue, then north on Washington Street, then east on Rose Place to Charles Street
   C. west on Roundsman Avenue, then north on Wolowski Street, then east on Trinity Place, then south on Charles Street to Rose Place
   D. east on Roundsman Avenue, then north on Charles Street to Rose Place

3. Police Officer Glasser is in an unmarked car at the intersection of Rose Place and Temple Street when he begins to follow two robbery suspects. The suspects go south for two blocks, then turn left for two blocks, then make another left turn for one more block. The suspects realize they are being followed and make a left turn and travel two more blocks and then make a right turn.
   In what direction are the suspects now headed?

   A. North   B. South   C. East   D. West

Questions 4-6.

DIRECTIONS: Questions 4 through 6 are to be answered SOLELY on the basis of the following map. The flow of traffic is indicated by the arrows. If there is only one arrow shown, then traffic flows only in the direction indicated by the arrow. If there are two arrows shown, then traffic flows in both directions. You must follow the flow of traffic.

4 (#1)

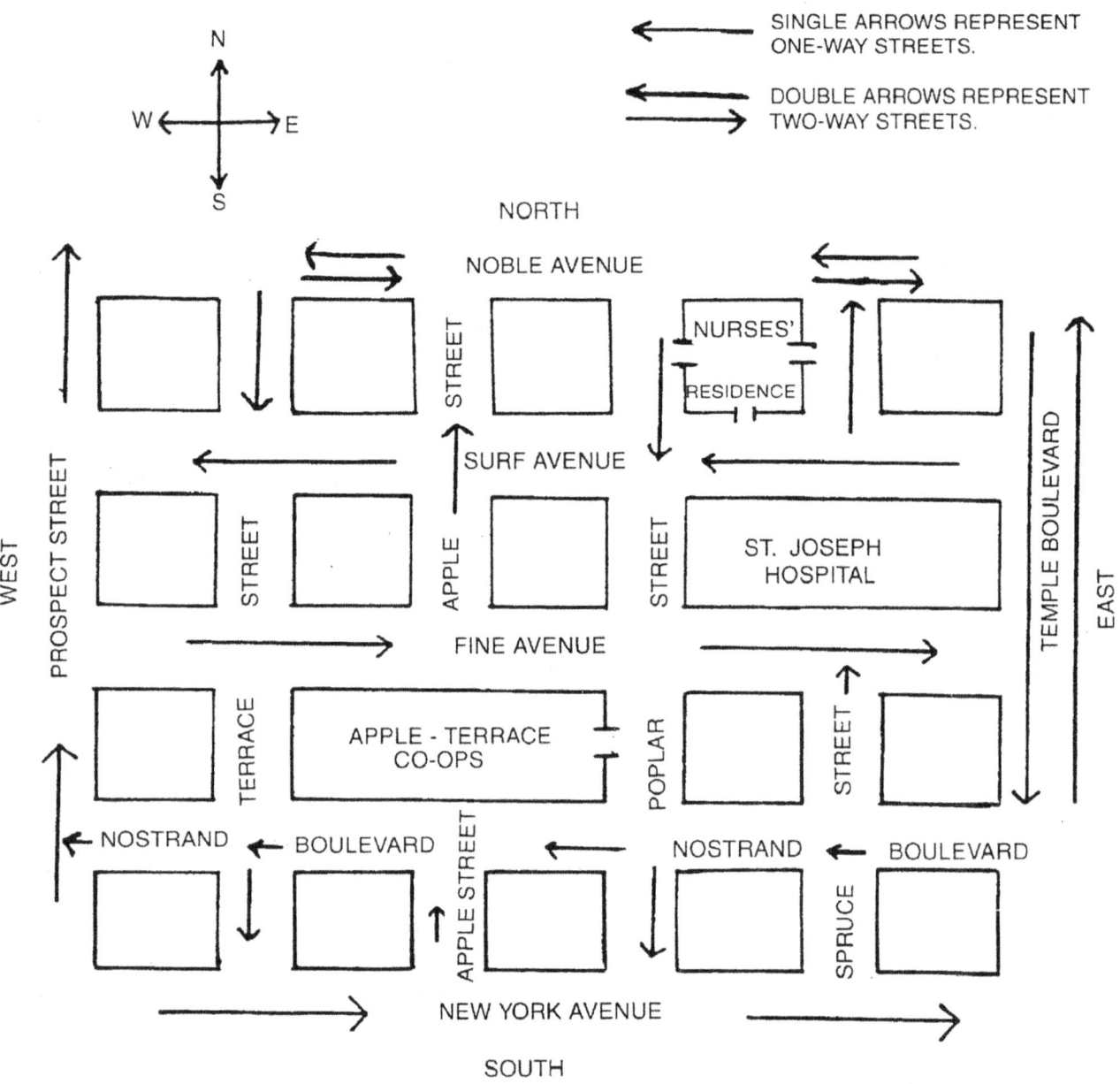

4. Police Officers Gannon and Vine are located at the intersection of Terrace Street and Surf Avenue when they receive a call from the radio dispatcher stating that they need to respond to an attempted murder at Spruce Street and Fine Avenue.
Which one of the following is the SHORTEST route for them to take in their patrol car, making sure to obey all traffic regulations?
Travel _____ to Spruce Street.

   A. west on Surf Avenue, then north on Prospect Street, then east on Noble Avenue, then south on Poplar Street, then east on Fine Avenue
   B. east on Surf Avenue, then south on Poplar Street, then east on Fine Avenue
   C. west on Surf Avenue, then south on Prospect Street, then east on Fine Avenue
   D. south on Terrace Street, then east on Fine Avenue

5. Police Officers Sears and Ronald are at Nostrand Boulevard and Prospect Street. They receive a call assigning them to investigate a disruptive group of youths at Temple Boulevard and Surf Avenue.
   Which one of the following is the SHORTEST route for them to take in their patrol car, making sure to obey all traffic regulations?
   Travel

   A. north on Prospect Street, then east on Surf Avenue to Temple Boulevard
   B. north on Prospect Street, then east on Noble Avenue, then south on Temple Boulevard to Surf Avenue
   C. north on Prospect Street, then east on Fine Avenue, then north on Temple Boulevard to Surf Avenue
   D. south on Prospect Street, then east on New York Avenue, then north on Temple Boulevard to Surf Avenue

6. While on patrol at Prospect Street and New York Avenue, Police Officers Ross and Rock are called to a burglary in progress near the entrance to the Apple-Terrace Co-ops on Poplar Street midway between Fine Avenue and Nostrand Boulevard.
   Which one of the following is the SHORTEST route for them to take in their patrol car, making sure to obey all traffic regulations?
   Travel _____ Poplar Street.

   A. east on New York Avenue, then north
   B. north on Prospect Avenue, then east on Fine Avenue, then south
   C. north on Prospect Street, then east on Surf Avenue, then south
   D. east on New York Avenue, then north on Temple Boulevard, then west on Surf Avenue, then south

Questions 7-8.

DIRECTIONS: Questions 7 and 8 are to be answered SOLELY on the basis of the map which appears below. The flow of traffic is indicated by the arrows. If there is only one arrow shown, then traffic flows only in the direction indicated by the arrow. If there are two arrows shown, then traffic flows in both directions. You must follow the flow of traffic.

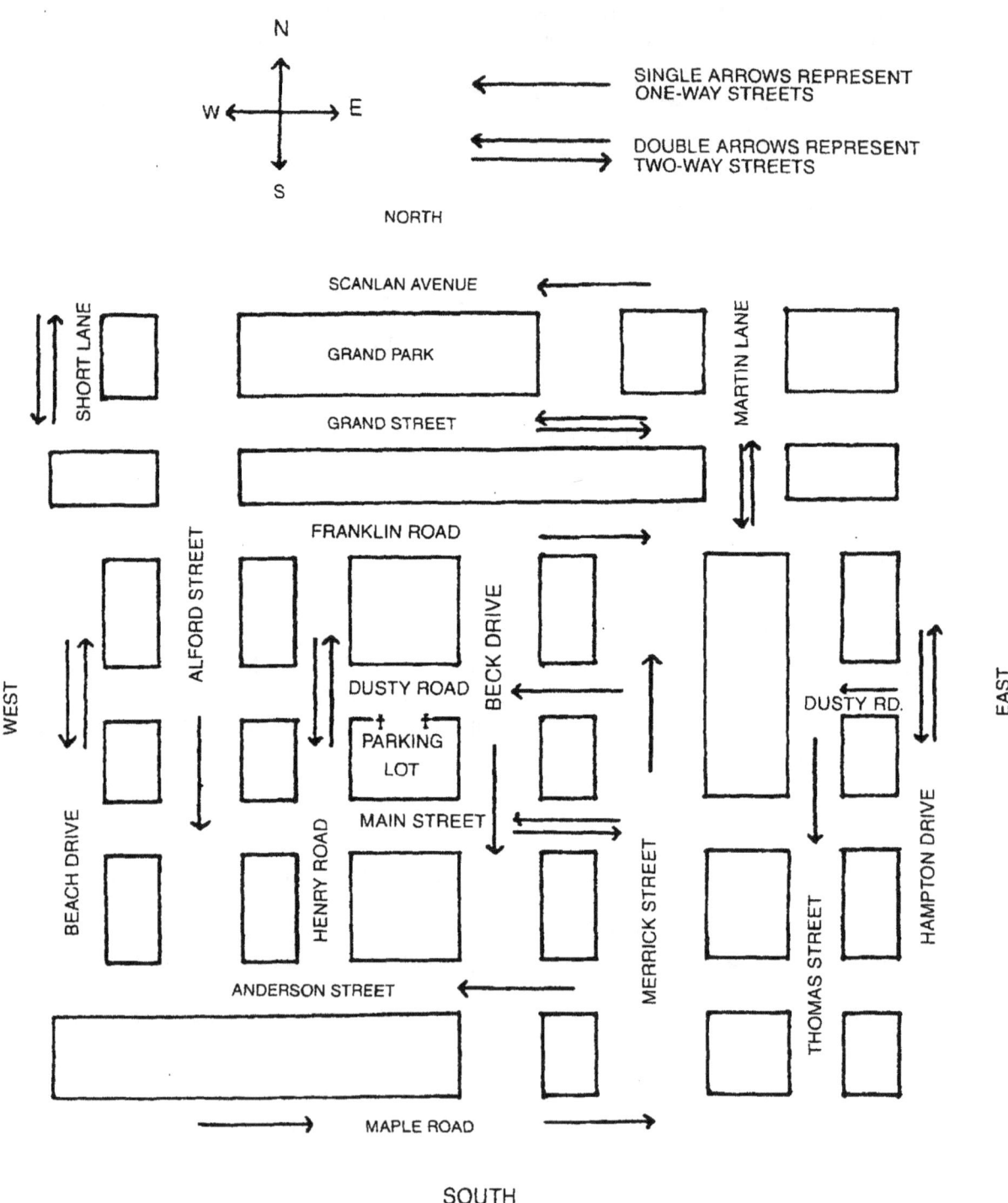

7. Police Officers Gold and Warren are at the intersection of Maple Road and Hampton Drive. The radio dispatcher has assigned them to investigate an attempted auto theft in the parking lot on Dusty Road.
Which one of the following is the SHORTEST route for the officers to take in their patrol car to get to the entrance of the parking lot on Dusty Road, making sure to obey all traffic regulations?
Travel _____ to the parking lot entrance.

7. ___

A. north on Hampton Drive, then west on Dusty Road
B. west on Maple Road, then north on Beck Drive, then west on Dusty Road
C. north on Hampton Drive, then west on Anderson Street, then north on Merrick Street, then west on Dusty Road
D. west on Maple Road, then north on Merrick Street, then west on Dusty Road

8. Police Officer Gladden is in a patrol car at the intersection of Beach Drive and Anderson Street when he spots a suspicious car. Police Officer Gladden calls the radio dispatcher to determine if the vehicle was stolen. Police Officer Gladden then follows the vehicle north on Beach Drive for three blocks, then turns right and proceeds for one block and makes another right. He then follows the vehicle for two blocks, and then they both make a left turn and continue driving. Police Officer Gladden now receives a call from the dispatcher stating the car was reported stolen and signals for the vehicle to pull to the side of the road.
In what direction was Police Officer Gladden heading at the time he signaled for the other car to pull over?

A. North   B. East   C. South   D. West

Questions 9-10.

DIRECTIONS: Questions 9 and 10 are to be answered SOLELY on the basis of the map which appears on the following page. The flow of traffic is indicated by the arrows. If there is only one arrow shown, then traffic flows only in the direction indicated by the arrow. If there are two arrows shown, then traffic flows in both directions. You must follow the flow of traffic.

8 (#1)

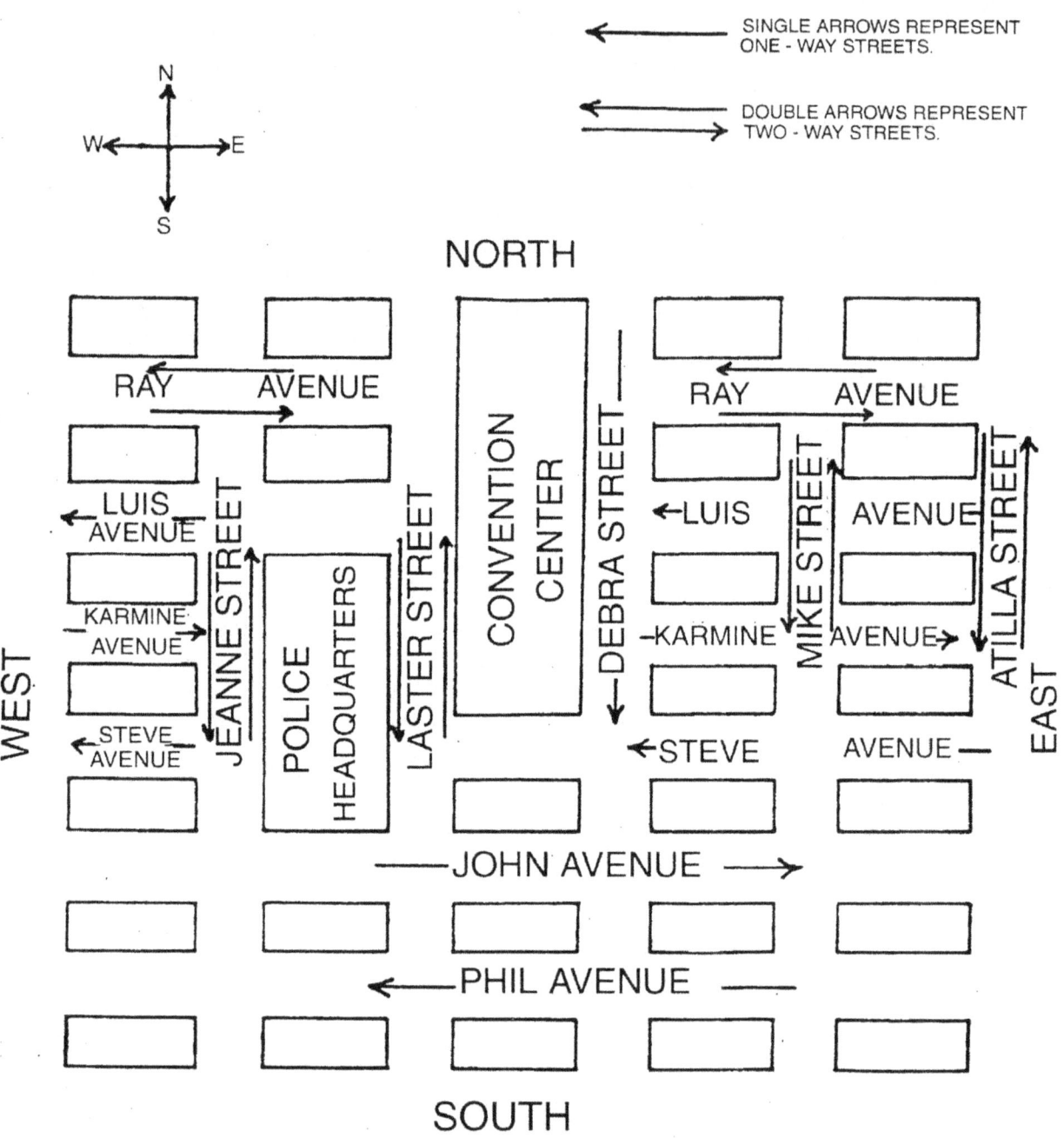

9. While in a patrol car located at Ray Avenue and Atilla Street, Police Officer Ashley receives a call from the dispatcher to respond to an assault at Jeanne Street and Karmine Avenue.
   Which one of the following is the SHORTEST route for Officer Ashley to follow in his patrol car, making sure to obey all traffic regulations?
   Travel

   A. south on Atilla Street, west on Luis Avenue, south on Debra Street, west on Steve Avenue, north on Lester Street, west on Luis Avenue, then one block south on Jeanne Street
   B. south on Atilla Street, then four blocks west on Phil Avenue, then north on Jeanne Street to Karmine Avenue

9. _____

C. west on Ray Avenue to Debra Street, then five blocks south to Phil Avenue, then west to Jeanne Street, then three blocks north to Karmine Avenue
D. south on Atilla Street, then four blocks west on John Avenue, then north on Jeanne Street to Karmine Avenue

10. After taking a complaint report from the assault victim, Officer Ashley receives a call from the dispatcher to respond to an auto larceny in progress at the corner of Debra Street and Luis Avenue.
Which one of the following is the SHORTEST route for Officer Ashley to follow in his patrol car, making sure to obey all traffic regulations?
Travel

A. south on Jeanne Street to John Avenue, then east three blocks on John Avenue, then north on Mike Street to Luis Avenue, then west to Debra Street
B. south on Jeanne Street to John Avenue, then east two blocks on John Avenue, then north on Debra Street to Luis Avenue
C. north on Jeanne Street two blocks, then east on Ray Avenue for one block, then south on Lester Street to Steve Avenue, then one block east on Steve Avenue, then north on Debra Street to Luis Avenue
D. south on Jeanne Street to John Avenue, then east on John Avenue to Atilla Street, then north three blocks to Luis Avenue, then west to Debra Street

Questions 11-13.

DIRECTIONS: Questions 11 through 13 are to be answered SOLELY on the basis of the following map. The flow of traffic is indicated by the arrows. You must follow the flow of traffic.

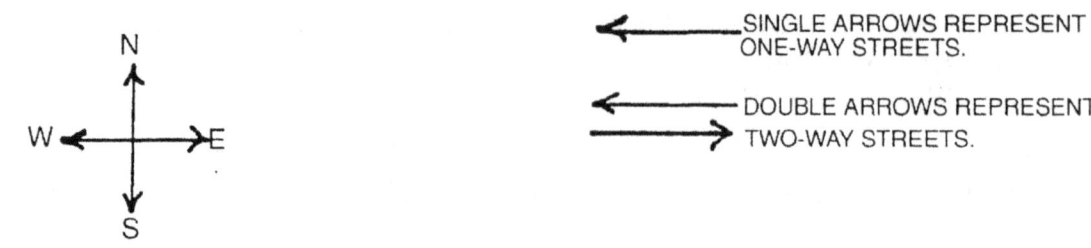

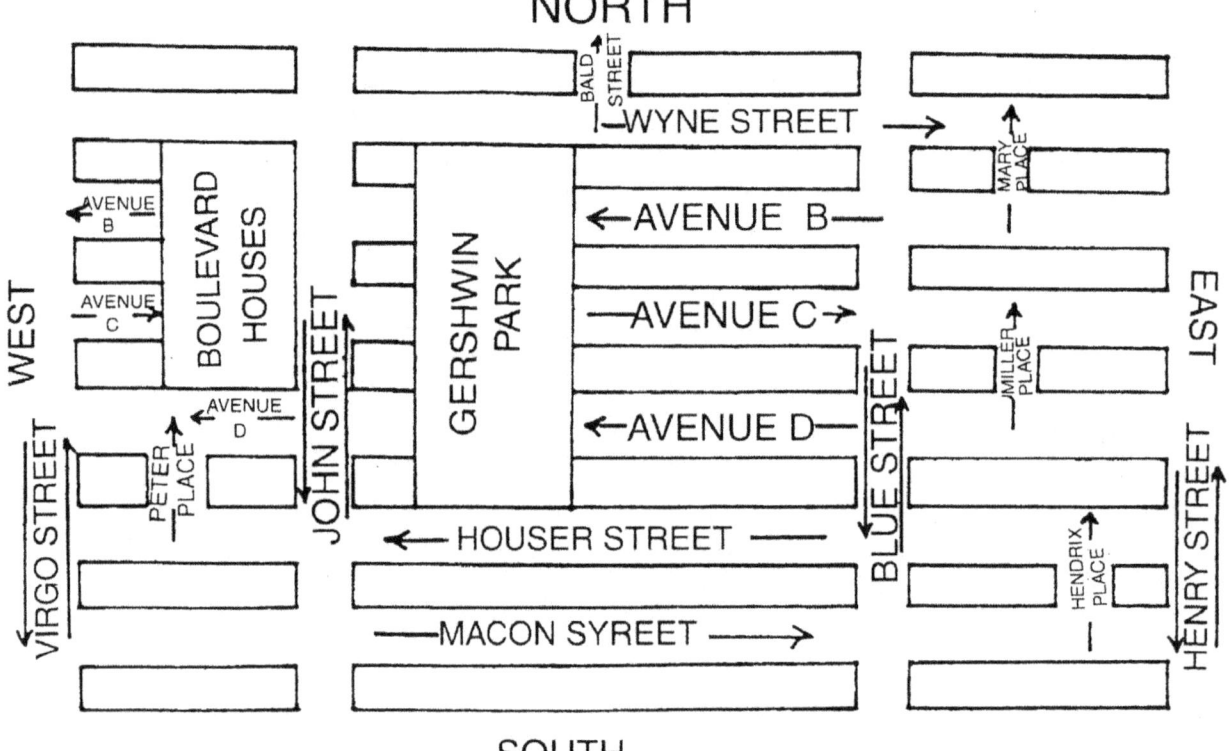

11. Police Officers Ranking and Fish are located at Wyne Street and John Street. The radio dispatcher has assigned them to investigate a motor vehicle accident at the corner of Henry Street and Houser Street.
Which one of the following is the SHORTEST route for them to take in their patrol car, making sure to obey all traffic regulations?
Travel

   A. four blocks south on John Street, then three blocks east on Houser Street to Henry Street
   B. two blocks east on Wyne Street, then two blocks south on Blue Street, then two blocks east on Avenue C, then two blocks south on Henry Street
   C. two blocks east on Wyne Street, then five blocks south on Blue Street, then two blocks east on Macon Street, then one block north on Henry Street
   D. five blocks south on John Street, then three blocks east on Macon Street, then one block north to Houser Street

12. Police Officers Rizzo and Latimer are located at Avenue B and Virgo Street. They respond to the scene of a robbery at Miller Place and Avenue D.
    Which one of the following is the SHORTEST route for them to take in their patrol car, making sure to obey all traffic regulations?
    Travel _____ to Miller Place.

    A. one block north on Virgo Street, then four blocks east on Wyne Street, then three blocks south on Henry Street, then one block west on Avenue D
    B. four blocks south on Virgo Street, then two blocks east on Macon Street, then two blocks north on Blue Street, then one block east on Avenue D
    C. three blocks south on Virgo Street, then east on Houser Street to Henry Street, then one block north on Henry Street, then one block west on Avenue D
    D. four blocks south on Virgo Street, then four blocks east to Henry Street, then north to Avenue D, then one block west

13. Police Officer Bendix is in an unmarked patrol car at the intersection of John Street and Macon Street when he begins to follow a robbery suspect. The suspect goes one block east, turns left, travels for three blocks, and then turns right. He drives for two blocks and then makes a right turn. In the middle of the block, the suspect realizes he is being followed and makes a u-turn. In what direction is the suspect now headed?

    A. North   B. South   C. East   D. West

Questions 14-15.

DIRECTIONS: Questions 14 and 15 are to be answered SOLELY on the basis of the following map. The flow of traffic is indicated by the arrows. If there is only one arrow shown, then traffic flows only in the direction indicated by the arrow. If there are two arrows shown, then traffic flows in both directions. You must follow the flow of traffic.

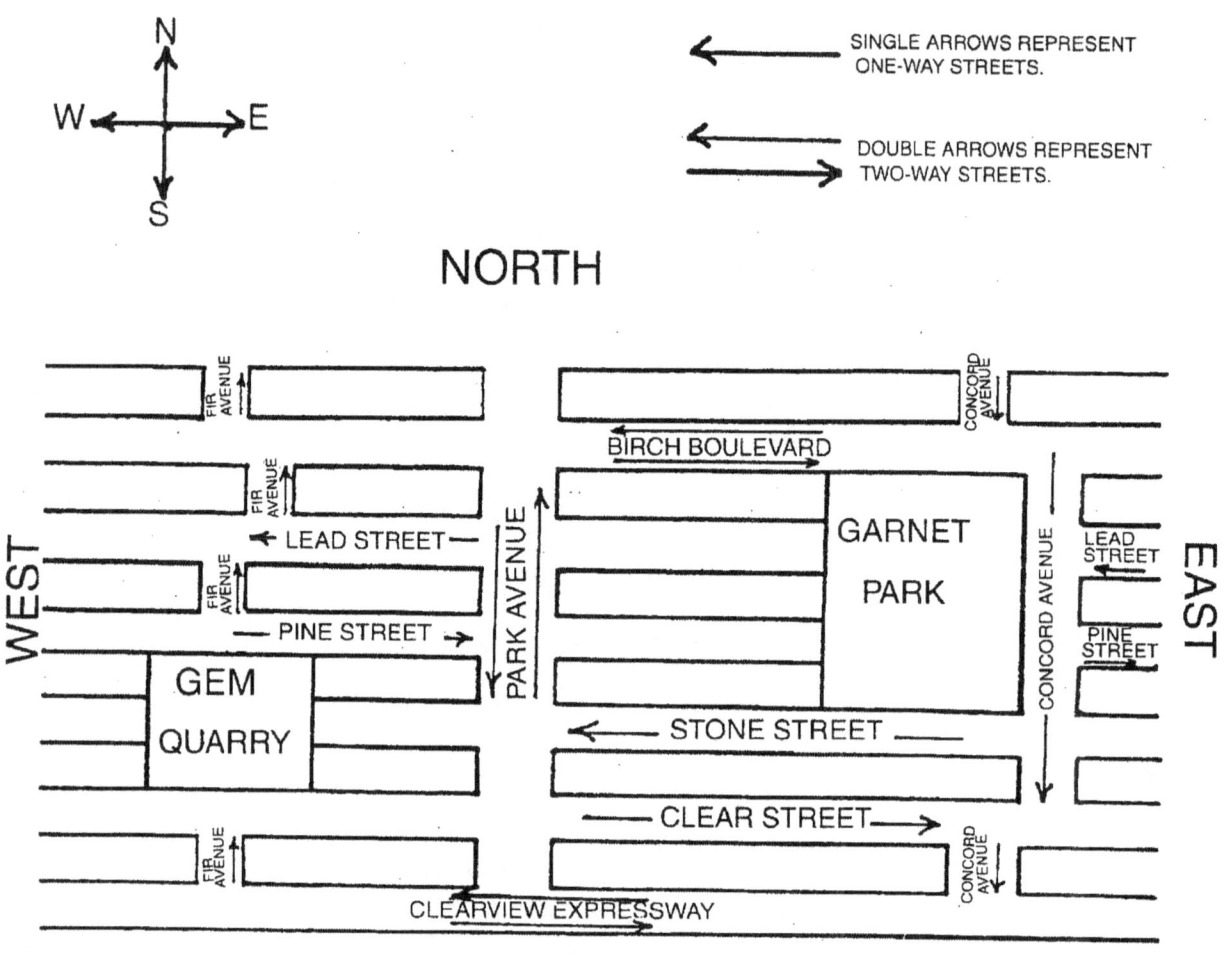

14. You are located at Fir Avenue and Birch Boulevard and receive a request to respond to a disturbance at Fir Avenue and Clear Street.
Which one of the following is the MOST direct route for you to take in your patrol car, making sure to obey all traffic regulations?
Travel

   A. one block east on Birch Boulevard, then four blocks south on Park Avenue, then one block east on Clear Street
   B. two blocks east on Birch Boulevard, then three blocks south on Concord Avenue, then two blocks west on Stone Street, then one block south on Park Avenue, then one block west on Clear Street
   C. one block east on Birch Boulevard, then five blocks south on Park Avenue, then one block west on the Clearview Expressway, then one block north on Fir Avenue
   D. two blocks south on Fir Avenue, then one block east on Pine Street, then three blocks south on Park Avenue, then one block east on the Clearview Expressway, then one block north on Fir Avenue

14. _____

15. You are located at the Clearview Expressway and Concord Avenue and receive a call to respond to a crime in progress at Concord Avenue and Pine Street. Which one of the following is the MOST direct route for you to take in your patrol car, making sure to obey all traffic regulations?
Travel

    A. two blocks west on the Clearview Expressway, then one block north on Fir Avenue, then one block east on Clear Street, then four blocks north on Park Avenue, then one block east on Birch Boulevard, then two blocks south on Concord Avenue
    B. one block north on Concord Avenue, then one block west on Clear Street, then one block north on Park Avenue, then one block east on Stone Street, then one block north on Concord Avenue
    C. one block west on the Clearview Expressway, then four blocks north on Park Avenue, then one block west on Lead Street, then one block south on Fir Avenue
    D. one block west on the Clearview Expressway, then five blocks north on Park Avenue, then one block east on Birch Boulevard, then two blocks south on Concord Avenue

15.____

Questions 16-20.

DIRECTIONS: Questions 16 through 20 are to be answered SOLELY on the basis of the following map. The flow of traffic is indicated by the arrows. You must follow the flow of traffic.

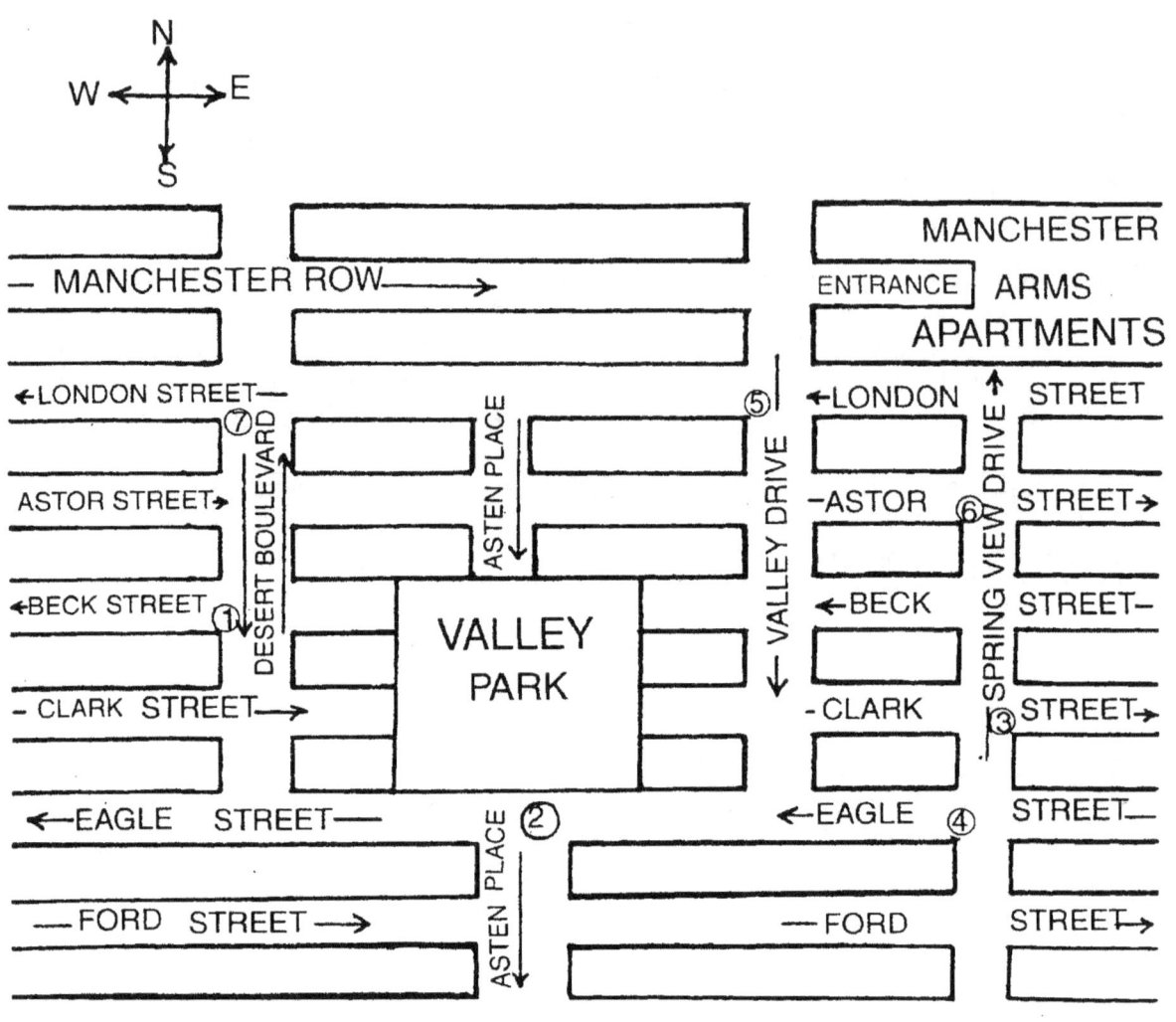

16. If you are located at Point 7 and travel south for one block, then turn east and travel two blocks, then turn south and travel two blocks, then turn east and travel one block, you will be CLOSEST to Point

   A. 2   B. 3   C. 4   D. 6

17. If you are located at Point 3 and travel north for one block, and then turn west and travel one block, and then turn south and travel two blocks, and then turn west and travel one block, you will be CLOSEST to Point

   A. 1   B. 2   C. 4   D. 6

18. You are located at Astor Street and Spring View Drive. You receive a call of a crime in progress at the intersection of Beck Street and Desert Boulevard.
   Which one of the following is the MOST direct route for you to take in your patrol car, making sure to obey all traffic regulations?
   Travel

   A. one block north on Spring View Drive, then three blocks west on London Street, then two blocks south on Desert Boulevard
   B. three blocks west on Astor Street, then one block south on Desert Boulevard

C. one block south on Spring View Drive, then three blocks west on Beck Street
D. three blocks south on Spring View Drive, then three blocks west on Eagle Street, then two blocks north on Desert Boulevard

19. You are located on Clark Street and Desert Boulevard and must respond to a disturbance at Clark Street and Spring View Drive.
Which one of the following is the MOST direct route for you to take in your patrol car, making sure to obey all traffic regulations?
Travel

   A. two blocks north on Desert Boulevard, then three blocks east on Astor Street, then two blocks south on Spring View Drive
   B. one block south on Desert Boulevard, then three blocks east on Eagle Street, then one block north on Spring View Drive
   C. two blocks north on Desert Boulevard, then two blocks east on Astor Street, then three blocks south on Valley Drive, then one block east on Eagle Street, then one block north on Spring View Drive
   D. two blocks north on Desert Boulevard, then two blocks east on Astor Street, then two blocks south on Valley Drive, then one block east on Clark Street

20. You are located at Valley Drive and Beck Street and receive a call to respond to the corner of Asten Place and Astor Street.
Which one of the following is the MOST direct route for you to take in your patrol car, making sure to obey all traffic regulations?
Travel _____ on Astor Street.

   A. one block north on Valley Drive, then one block west
   B. two blocks south on Valley Drive, then one block east on Eagle Street, then three blocks north on Spring View Drive, then two blocks west
   C. two blocks south on Valley Drive, then two blocks west on Eagle Street, then three blocks north on Desert Boulevard, then one block east
   D. one block south on Valley Drive, then one block east on Clark Street, then two blocks north on Spring View Drive, then two blocks west

KEY (CORRECT ANSWERS)

1.	C	11.	B
2.	A	12.	A
3.	A	13.	A
4.	D	14.	C
5.	C	15.	D
6.	B	16.	B
7.	C	17.	B
8.	B	18.	A
9.	A	19.	D
10.	A	20.	C

READING COMPREHENSION
UNDERSTANDING AND INTERPRETING WRITTEN MATERIAL
EXAMINATION SECTION
TEST 1

DIRECTIONS: Each question or incomplete statement is followed by several suggested answers or completions. Select the one that BEST answers the question or completes the statement. *PRINT THE LETTER OF THE CORRECT ANSWER IN THE SPACE AT THE RIGHT.*

Questions 1-4.

DIRECTIONS: Questions 1 through 4 are to be answered SOLELY on the basis of the following passage.

On April 6, at 5:25 A.M., while patrolling the #8 train southbound to Brooklyn, Transit Police Officer O'Rourke noticed a young woman at the end of the car who appeared to be ill. Officer O'Rourke approached the woman and asked her if she was feeling all right. The woman was crying and began speaking incoherently. Officer O'Rourke escorted the woman off the train at the next southbound #8 platform in order to obtain information from her. After speaking with her for fifteen minutes, Officer O'Rourke learned that her name was Carol Rivers and that she had been assaulted and sexually molested while waiting for the southbound #8 train about a half hour before meeting the Officer. Miss Rivers described the suspect as a white male, in his forties, with gray hair, glasses, a red shirt, black pants, and a brown hat. The suspect fled on a northbound #8 train with the victim's pocketbook. Officer O'Rourke then radioed for an ambulance to respond to the location to assist Miss Rivers.

The next day at approximately 5:30 A.M., while Officer O'Rourke was standing on the subway platform waiting to board the uptown #7 train to Queens, he noticed an individual coming down the steps from the southbound platform. The man was in his forties, with gray hair, dark glasses, and the same clothing described by Miss Rivers the day before, except for his shirt, which was white. Officer O'Rourke, believing the man to be the same perpetrator, decided to follow him in order to observe the suspect's actions. The man was walking alongside a woman on the northbound platform and attempted to snatch her pocketbook. The woman held onto her purse and started to yell for the police. The man immediately released his hold on the pocketbook and ran down the platform onto an awaiting #7 train to Manhattan. Officer O'Rourke pursued the man onto the train and subsequently placed him under arrest two stations later.

1. Officer O'Rourke requested that the ambulance respond to the subway platform of the _____ train. 1._____

   A. northbound # 8   B. uptown # 7
   C. downtown # 7   D. southbound # 8

2. At approximately what time was Miss Rivers assaulted? _____ A.M. 2._____

   A. 4:55   B. 5:10   C. 5:25   D. 5:40

3. The suspect arrested by Officer O'Rourke was wearing a shirt _____ and _____ pants.

   A. red; blue
   B. white; black
   C. red; black
   D. white; red

4. On April 7, Officer O'Rourke boarded a train to

   A. Manhattan
   B. Queens
   C. the Bronx
   D. Brooklyn

Questions 5-7.

DIRECTIONS: Questions 5 through 7 are to be answered SOLELY on the basis of the following passage.

Police Officers Ryder and Brown respond to a call concerning a past burglary in a private house located at 1296 Brentwood Road. When the Officers arrive, they are met by William Parker, who owns the house. Mr. Parker tells the Officers that he had been out of town for the entire weekend and, upon his return twenty minutes ago, discovered that the lock on his back door was broken. He also discovered that several items were missing from around his house. At this point, Officer Ryder asks Mr. Parker to show her where the burglars entered. Meanwhile, Officer Brown makes a search of the immediate area. Officer Ryder's investigation reveals that the burglars had cut a wire located by the front basement window in order to disable the alarm system. The burglars then forced open the lock with a metal bar of some kind. Officer Brown's search of the area uncovers no evidence. Officer Ryder then asks Mr. Parker to describe the items which are missing. Mr. Parker says that his 19" plasma television and clock radio are gone, along with several items which were borrowed from various friends. Among the missing items are a compact disc player owned by David Mills, a videotape recorder owned by Samantha Burns, and a portable tape player with headphones owned by Roger Denning. Officer Ryder lists the missing items and the owners' names in her report and tells Mr. Parker to call the station house in the morning to obtain a report number which he can use if he files an insurance claim.

5. The thieves broke the lock of which entrance?

   A. Side   B. Front   C. Basement   D. Back

6. Which of the missing items were owned by William Parker?

   A. Color television and clock radio
   B. Compact disc player and tape player
   C. Videotape recorder and compact disc player
   D. Portable tape player and headphones

7. What crime is this passage PRIMARILY concerned with?

   A. Arson   B. Assault   C. Burglary   D. Fraud

Questions 8-10.

DIRECTIONS: Questions 8 through 10 are to be answered SOLELY on the basis of the following passage.

Police Officers Wilson and Mills receive a radio call to investigate an auto accident involving injuries. Upon their arrival, Officer Mills approaches a Mustang convertible which had been driven into the side of an Oldsmobile sedan. There is also a small Dodge truck several feet away which had crashed into a fire hydrant. Officer Mills immediately determines that no one is injured and radios the dispatcher to cancel the ambulance. Meanwhile, Officer Wilson interviews Sam Thomas, who is the owner and driver of the Mustang. Mr. Thomas states that he was driving south on Bedford Avenue when a large Oldsmobile pulled out of a parking lot in front of him. Mr. Thomas goes on to say that he immediately hit his brakes but slid into the side of the Oldsmobile. Officer Mills interviews Thomas Parker, who is the driver of the Oldsmobile. Mr. Parker admits that he drove out of the parking lot without looking for oncoming traffic. He tells Officer Mills that he is not used to driving and borrowed the Oldsmobile from his brother, Harold Parker, who is the owner of the car. Finally, Officer Wilson interviews Rutger Schmidt, who is the driver of the Dodge truck. Mr. Schmidt indicates that, in an attempt to avoid the accident, he swerved out of the way, lost control of the truck, and ran into a fire hydrant. Mr. Schmidt tells Officer Wilson that he works for the Acme Exterminating Company, which owns the truck. Following the interviews, the two Officers write their accident report and indicate the damage to each vehicle. The Mustang had a damaged front bumper and grill, and broken headlights; the Oldsmobile had a dented driver's side quarter panel; the Dodge truck had a crumpled bumper and blown right front tire.

8. Who was the owner of the Oldsmobile sedan?

    A. Sam Thomas
    B. Thomas Parker
    C. Harold Parker
    D. Rutger Schmidt

9. What was damaged on the Dodge truck?

    A. Driver's side quarter panel
    B. Bumper and right front tire
    C. Tailgate and tail lights
    D. Front bumper, grill, and headlights

10. The driver of which vehicle was the PRIMARY cause of the accident?

    A. Mustang convertible
    B. Patrol car
    C. Dodge truck
    D. Oldsmobile sedan

Questions 11-13.

DIRECTIONS: Questions 11 through 13 are to be answered SOLELY on the basis of the following passage.

Police Officer Lombardo was dispatched to the scene of an apparently dead human body. His supervisor and another Officer were at the scene, as were two paramedics. The paramedics, Pete Lizzo and Erick Clark, had just pronounced the body dead at 6:55 P.M. There were no relatives present, and a neighbor, Eddie Torres, told Officer Lombardo that the dead person lived alone and had no family. Mr. Torres agreed to be a witness to the search of the premises. Officer Lombardo knew that the police were required to voucher or hold all valuables and important papers for safekeeping if a close relative did not live with the dead person. The apartment was filled with a large number of possessions, including two gold rings, a gold watch, $200 in cash, and kitchen and living room furniture. They also found an old black and white television set, old clothing, and numerous kitchen utensils. In a tin box, the Officer found a birth certificate, social security card, and the dead person's diary. After the search was completed, the jewelry, cash, birth certificate, and social security card were vouchered. Eddie Torres signed Officer Lombardo's Memo Book.

11. Of the following, which items were vouchered by Officer Lombardo?

    A. Two gold rings, a gold watch, a social security card, birth certificate, and $200 in cash
    B. A gold watch, two gold rings, $200 cash, a diary, and a social security card
    C. A birth certificate, social security card, diary, jewelry, and $200 in cash
    D. A social security card, two gold watches, a gold ring, a birth certificate, and $200 cash

12. The search was witnessed by a

    A. neighbor
    B. relative
    C. police officer
    D. paramedic

13. Officer Lombardo vouchered the dead person's property because

    A. the paramedics were present
    B. a supervisor was not available
    C. there was only one witness
    D. there was no relative living with the dead person

Question 14.

DIRECTIONS: Question 14 pertains to the following section of the Penal Law.

A person who, after having been three times convicted within this state, of felonies or attempts to commit felonies, or under the law of any other state, government or country, of crimes which if committed within this state would be felonious, commits a felony, other than murder, first or second degree, or treason, within this state, shall be sentenced upon conviction of such fourth, or subsequent offense to imprisonment in a state prison for an indeterminate term the minimum of which shall be not less than the maximum term provided for first offenders for the crime for which the individual has been convicted but, in any event, the minimum term upon conviction for a felony as the fourth or subsequent offense, shall be not less than fifteen years, and the maximum thereof shall be his natural life.

14. Under the terms of the above quoted portion of the section of the Penal Law a person must receive the increased punishment therein provided, if

    A. he is convicted of a felony and has been three times previously convicted of felonies
    B. he has been three times previously convicted of felonies, regardless of the nature of his present conviction
    C. his fourth conviction is for murder, first or second degree, or treason
    D. he has previously been convicted three times of murder, first or second degree, or treason

Questions 15-17.

DIRECTIONS: Questions 15 through 17 are to be answered SOLELY on the basis of the following passage.

At 11:30 P.M., while parked in front of 945 Howard Street, Police Officers Abbott and Johnson received a radio call of a family dispute at 779 Seward Street, Apartment 1928. The radio dispatcher informed the Officers that the call came from Mrs. Debra Lacoste who lives in Apartment 1930. The Officers arrived at the location and heard yelling and screaming. When the Officers knocked on the door, a woman crying hysterically opened the door. The woman, Gloria Ross, informed the Officers that her husband, Sam Ross, was in her apartment. She said he was drunk, had yelled at her, and had made threats to hurt her if she did not let him see his children. Mrs. Ross then presented a letter to Officer Abbott, which he recognized as being an Order of Protection issued by Family Court. The Order of Protection stated that Mr. Ross was not to be seen anywhere near his wife, including her residence and place of employment. Furthermore, the Order stated that he had no right to see the children or to yell at his wife or use obscene language in his wife's presence. Mrs. Ross told the Officer that she wanted her husband arrested for violating the Order of Protection. Officer Johnson quickly read the Order of Protection and informed Officer Abbott that the Order was valid. Officer Abbott ordered Sam Ross to turn around with his hands behind his back, and Officer Abbott handcuffed him and placed him under arrest.

15. Which of the following persons FIRST made the authorities aware of the family dispute? 15._____

   A. A neighbor
   B. The victim
   C. A police officer
   D. The suspect

16. The Police Officers responded to a report of a disturbance at _____ Street, Apartment _____. 16._____

   A. 945 Howard; 1928
   B. 779 Seward; 1930
   C. 779 Seward; 1928
   D. 945 Howard; 1930

17. Which of the following actions caused Mr. Ross to be arrested? He 17._____

   A. called his children on the telephone
   B. tried to visit his children
   C. waited for his wife in front of her job
   D. yelled at his children

Questions 18-19.

DIRECTIONS: Questions 18 and 19 are to be answered SOLELY on the basis of the following passage.

As a result of numerous interviews of complainants and witnesses of violent crimes, Officer Wells has noticed a serious rise in the number of certain crimes in his patrol area over the past three months. He has observed that most of the rapes take place on E. 98th Street between Lott Avenue and Herk Place; assaults happen on Lott Avenue between Chester Avenue and E. 98th Street; and the majority of the robberies occur on Lott Avenue between E. 98th Street and Hughes Place. The assaults take place between 1:00 A.M. and 3:00 A.M. All of the robberies happen between 1:00 A.M. and 6:00 A.M., and most of the rapes happen between 8:00 A.M. and 11:00 A.M. The rapes usually occur on Mondays and Wednesdays, the robberies oh Fridays and Saturdays, and the assaults on Saturdays and Sundays.

18. Officer Wells would MOST effectively reduce the number of robberies by patrolling   18._____

    A. Lott Avenue between E. 98th Street and Hughes Place on Fridays and Saturdays between 1:00 A.M. and 8:00 A.M.
    B. Lott Avenue between E. 98th Street and Chester Avenue on Saturdays and Sundays between 1:00 A.M. and 6:00 A.M.
    C. E. 98th Street between Lott Avenue and Herk Place on Saturdays and Sundays between 1:00 A.M. and 3:00 A.M.
    D. E. 98th Street between Herk Place and Chester Avenue on Mondays and Wednesdays between 8:00 A.M. and 11:00 A.M.

19. Officer Wells has been informed by his supervisor that he will be assigned to a patrol   19._____
    each week that would allow him to concentrate on reducing the number of rapes. What would be the MOST appropriate patrol for Officer Wells to work?

    A. Tuesday through Saturday, 8:00 P.M. to 4:00 P.M.
    B. Monday through Friday, 7:30 A.M. to 3:30 P.M.
    C. Wednesday through Sunday, noon to 8:00 P.M.
    D. Monday through Friday, 3:00 P.M. to 11:00 P.M.

Questions 20-23.

DIRECTIONS: Questions 20 through 23 are to be answered SOLELY on the basis of the following passage.

Police Officers Grice and Sexton were working a 4:00 P.M. to Midnight tour of duty on Friday, December 5, when they were assigned to investigate a burglary. They were told to respond to 355 Grand Street, the 14th floor, Apartment 1402, and to speak to the complainant, Ms. Starr. Upon arrival, Officer Sexton interviewed Ms. Starr, who stated that when she returned home from work at approximately 6:10 P.M., she was unable to unlock her door because the keyhole had been stuffed with toothpicks. After the door was opened by building maintenance, she entered her apartment and saw that her jewelry box had been emptied and was laying on the floor.

Officer Grice, who is qualified in the recovery of fingerprints, dusted the jewelry box and the front door in an attempt to recover any fingerprints that the burglar may have left. The Officers also interviewed Mrs. Caputo, who lives in Apartment 1404, and Mr. Babbit, who lives in Apartment 1407. Both individuals stated that they neither saw nor heard anything unusual.

The next night, Saturday, December 6, Officers Grice and Sexton responded to Apartment 1514 in the same building on a call of a burglary. The complainant, Ms. Chung, stated that when she returned home from shopping she discovered that her lock had been stuffed with chewing gum and that her apartment had been burglarized. Officer Grice dusted the front door and a dresser, which had been opened, for prints.

Ten days after the last burglary, Detective Carrano, who had been assigned to investigate the burglaries, was informed by Mr. Hunt of the fingerprint identification unit that the prints recovered from both apartments belonged to Peter Remo of 355 Gravel Street, Apartment 1705. Later that evening, after obtaining an arrest warrant, Detective Carrano arrested Peter Remo for the burglaries.

20. Who lived on the same floor as Ms. Starr?

    A. Ms. Chung   B. Peter Remo
    C. Mr. Babbit   D. Mr. Hunt

21. Who was responsible for recovering the fingerprints that were used to identify Peter Remo?

    A. Officer Grice   B. Mr. Hunt
    C. Detective Carrano   D. Officer Sexton

22. When was Peter Remo arrested? December

    A. 5   B. 6   C. 15   D. 16

23. Why was Ms. Starr unable to unlock her door?

    A. She lost her keys.
    B. Chewing gum had been stuffed into the lock.
    C. Her keys had been taken from her jewelry box.
    D. The lock was stuffed with toothpicks.

Questions 24-25.

DIRECTIONS: Questions 24 and 25 are to be answered SOLELY on the basis of the following passage.

While working an 8:00 A.M. to 4:00 P.M. shift on January 14, Police Officers Jones and Smith received a radio call at 1:45 P.M. to investigate a report of a man with a gun in front of 103 Lexington Avenue. Mary Holmes had called 911 from her home at 1:43 P.M. and explained that two days ago while on her way home from work, she had been threatened by a man with a gun in front of her home at 113 Lowell Street. She told the police operator that the same man was now standing in front of Harry's Lounge at 103 Lexington Avenue, drinking a beer. She described him as being 30-40 years old, 5'6", 160 lbs., wearing a gray coat, gray brim hat, and gold wire-rimmed glasses. The Officers responded to the location and observed a male fitting the description given by Miss Holmes. The Officers approached the suspect and, while searching his right front waistband, Officer Jones found a chromeplated .38 caliber revolver licensed and registered under the name of Joseph Fitz. Miss Holmes was brought to the scene and identified the suspect as the person who had threatened her earlier. Officer Smith then placed the man, identified as Joseph Fitz, under arrest.

24. On what day did the suspect threaten Miss Holmes? January

    A. 10   B. 12   C. 14   D. 16

25. Officer Jones recovered the gun from the suspect's waistband.

    A. left front   B. right rear
    C. left rear   D. right front

KEY (CORRECT ANSWERS)

1.	D	11.	A
2.	A	12.	A
3.	B	13.	D
4.	A	14.	A
5.	D	15.	A
6.	A	16.	C
7.	C	17.	B
8.	C	18.	A
9.	B	19.	B
10.	D	20.	C

21. A
22. D
23. D
24. B
25. D

TEST 2

DIRECTIONS: Each question or incomplete statement is followed by several suggested answers or completions. Select the one that BEST answers the question or completes the statement. *PRINT THE LETTER OF THE CORRECT ANSWER IN THE SPACE AT THE RIGHT.*

Questions 1-4.

DIRECTIONS: Questions 1 through 4 are to be answered SOLELY on the basis of the following passage.

On May 10, at 5:30 P.M., Police Officers Swift and Monroe were on routine patrol when they were dispatched to 1180 Albany Avenue, Apartment 3C, on an assault in progress. They arrived at the apartment at 5:40 P.M. and were met by Mr. Raymond Ambrose. Mr. Ambrose said he called the police because he heard yelling and screaming coming from Apartment 3A, but it had since stopped. Mr. Ambrose told the Officers that the tenant in 3A, Helen Gray, lived alone ever since her divorce.

Officer Monroe knocked on the door of Apartment 3A and noticed that the door was partially opened. The Officers cautiously entered the apartment, which appeared to have been ransacked. Officer Swift checked the fire escape while his partner searched the bedroom, where he found Mrs. Gray, unconscious, lying on the floor and bleeding heavily from the head. A blood-covered baseball bat was found next to her. The Officer called for an ambulance to respond while Officer Swift tried to gather information from neighbors.

Mary Grable, age 68, of Apartment 3B, Ben Grim, age 16 of Apartment 1A, and Angela Arnold, age 27, of 1162 Albany Avenue were standing in the hallway. Ms. Arnold stated that she and Mrs. Gray are close friends, and she became concerned when she saw Stuart Gray in the neighborhood around 5:10 P.M. Ms. Arnold told Officer Swift, *Since they've been divorced, Stuart visits Helen to get money to support a "crack" habit, and it always leads to an argument.* Grable said she heard a commotion, but didn't know who was involved. Grim told Officer Swift that he saw Stuart Gray running from the building at about 5:35 P.M. with blood on his hands and shirt.

Paramedics arrived at 5:50 P.M. and transported Mrs. Gray to the hospital, where she died at 6:30 P.M. without regaining consciousness. Stuart Gray was arrested at 7:15 the next morning at the home of his mother, Valerie Gray, and was charged with the homicide.

1. From the information given, it is MOST likely that the crime was committed between   1._____
   A. 5:10 A.M. - 5:35 A.M.   B. 5:10 P.M. - 5:35 P.M.
   C. 5:30 P.M. - 5:35 P.M.   D. 5:30 P.M. - 5:50 P.M.

2. Who was the FIRST person to find Mrs. Gray?   2._____
   A. Officer Monroe   B. Mr. Ambrose
   C. Officer Swift   D. Ms. Arnold

3. Whose information tied Stuart to the crime?   3._____
   A. Ms. Arnold and Ben Grim   B. Mr. Ambrose and Ms. Arnold
   C. Ben Grim and Valerie Gray   D. Ms. Arnold and Ms. Grable

4. Stuart Gray was arrested on May

   A. 10 at 6:30 P.M.
   B. 11 at 7:15 P.M.
   C. 10 at 7:15 A.M.
   D. 11 at 7:15 A.M

Questions 5-8.

DIRECTIONS: Questions 5 through 8 are to be answered SOLELY on the basis of the following passage.

While returning to the 15th Precinct from court, Police Officer Moody encountered an armed robbery in progress outside of 238 Madison Street. When the perpetrator saw the Officer, he fled into the building and attempted to enter the second floor apartment of Maria Vasquez. Ms. Vasquez had previously opened the door when she heard the noise downstairs. When Ms. Vasquez saw the perpetrator approaching her with a gun in his hand, she immediately closed and locked the door. Since the perpetrator was not able to gain entrance to the apartment, he jumped out of the hallway window and hid in the courtyard. When Officer Moody arrived at the bottom of the second floor stairway, he heard Ms. Vasquez crying hysterically from inside the apartment. He banged on the door and called to her to see if she was all right. Ms. Vasquez did not speak English and, thinking it was the perpetrator, she refused to open the door. As a result, Officer Moody assumed that the woman was being held hostage by the perpetrator. Officer Moody immediately stepped away from the door, advised the radio dispatcher of the circumstances, and requested back-up assistance.

Every sector car in the precinct responded to assist Officer Moody; and each, with the exception of sectors Adam and Charlie, took up a strategic location outside of the building. Officers O'Connor and Torres, of sector Adam, went up to the second floor to guard the apartment door with Officer Moody. Officer Perez, of sector Charlie, went up to the roof. Officer Donadio, also of sector Charlie, started to enter the courtyard when he observed the perpetrator hiding in the bushes. Officer Donadio quickly took cover behind the cement wall entrance of the courtyard and ordered the perpetrator at gunpoint to surrender. The perpetrator surrendered his weapon and allowed himself to be easily apprehended. Officer Donadio then advised the other Officers by radio that the perpetrator was in custody and that Ms. Vasquez was not being held hostage.

5. Which Officer went up to the roof?

   A. O'Connor   B. Perez   C. Donadio   D. Moody

6. Officer Moody chased the perpetrator because he

   A. was trying to get into the apartment of Maria Vasquez
   B. was holding Maria Vasquez hostage
   C. was attempting to commit an armed robbery
   D. jumped out the second floor hallway window

7. Which Officer was NOT on the second floor?

   A. Moody   B. Torres   C. O'Connor   D. Donadio

8. While Officer Moody was standing at the bottom of the stairs, the suspect was

   A. in Ms. Vasquez's apartment
   B. in the courtyard
   C. on the roof
   D. on the second floor fire escape

Questions 9-11.

DIRECTIONS: Questions 9 through 11 are to be answered SOLELY on the basis of the following passage.

Police Officer Berman has been assigned to a steady post from Hartman Boulevard to Bement Street on Forest Avenue for the past two years. Officer Berman's duties involve walking along Forest Avenue and in and out of stores talking with the people on his post to ensure that everything is all right. While on duty at 11:30 on Saturday morning, Officer Berman walks into Pete Arturo's Boutique, which is normally filled with female customers because of the type of merchandise sold there. Today, the Officer sees only three young men in the store. Officer Berman looks around and notices that Pete is not in sight. Officer Berman notices a thin man whom he has never seen behind the register. Officer Berman decides to ask for Mrs. Arturo, knowing that Pete is not married, because he suspects that something is wrong. The thin man replies with a smile, *She will be in a little later.* Officer Berman then walks out of the boutique and calls for back-up assistance on a possible robbery in progress. At 11:40, Police Officers Fernandez and Heck arrive at the side of Arturo's Boutique. Five minutes later, Police Officer Jones arrives in his scooter. The Officers are now waiting for a Supervisor to arrive so they can proceed with the plan of action, which they have already discussed. Two minutes after Officer Jones arrives, Sgt. Demond pulls up with his driver, Police Officer Ricco, and gathers all of the information. Sgt. Demond then calls the boutique by phone, identifies himself, and advises the man who answers to give himself up so that nobody will get hurt. Sgt. Demond also tells the man on the phone that he has the store surrounded and will give them five minutes to surrender. The three men walk out of the boutique with Mr. Arturo, who is unharmed. Officer Berman recovers three loaded .38 caliber revolvers from the suspects.

9. How many police personnel responded to Officer Berman's call for assistance?

   A. Four   B. Five   C. Six   D. Seven

10. At what time did Sergeant Demond arrive at the boutique? _____ A.M.

    A. 11:40   B. 11:42   C. 11:45   D. 11:47

11. Which of the following Officers arrived in the scooter?

    A. Berman   B. Fernandez   C. Jones   D. Heck

Questions 12-14.

DIRECTIONS: Questions 12 through 14 are to be answered SOLELY on the basis of the following passage.

Police Officer Smith was reassigned to the Parkhill Housing Complex, which consists of nine 8-story buildings. He was told that nine rapes had occurred in the last eight days in the complex and all had taken place between 9:00 A.M. and 6:00 P.M. On May 2, Officer Smith was working the 10:00 A.M. to 6:00 P.M. shift. At the beginning of Officer Smith's shift, his Supervisor, Sergeant Larry, gave him the suspected rapist's description, which had been obtained on April 27 from Nancy Lewis, one of the rape victims. The suspect was described as a male, Black, 6'2", approximately 210 lbs., having a light complexion and the word *Budda* tattooed on his left forearm.

While on patrol several blocks from the Parkhill Complex at Noon of the same day, Officer Smith was called by the dispatcher and told to respond to a complaint at 110 Park Avenue, Apartment 3C, located in the complex. Upon his arrival at the apartment, he was met by Mary Wilson, who told him that her 16-year-old daughter Tammy had just been raped in the building elevator. Tammy stated that when she entered her building, a Black male, approximately 26 years old, about 6'1", wearing a suit, had been waiting for the elevator. She also told Officer Smith that when she entered the elevator with this man, he forced her to the floor, raped her, and pushed her out of the elevator on the 7th floor.

On May 3, at 8:00 A.M., an individual fitting the description given by Ms. Lewis was apprehended in front of 55 Hill Street, another building in the Parkhill Complex. The suspect's name was John Jones. At 12:30 P.M. of the same day, Ms. Wilson and Ms. Lewis went to the precinct station house and identified John Jones as the person who raped them.

12. Who was the FIRST person to give Officer Smith a description of the rapist?

    A. Sergeant Larry
    B. Tammy Wilson
    C. Mary Wilson
    D. Nancy Lewis

13. Where was Tammy Wilson raped?

    A. In the elevator at 55 Hill Street
    B. On the 5th floor at 110 Park Avenue
    C. In the elevator at 110 Park Avenue
    D. On the 7th floor at 55 Hill Street

14. John Jones was apprehended the

    A. same day as the rape of Nancy Lewis
    B. day after the rape of Nancy Lewis
    C. same day as the rape of Tammy Wilson
    D. day after the rape of Tammy Wilson

Questions 15-17.

DIRECTIONS: Questions 15 through 17 are to be answered SOLELY on the basis of the following passage.

Police Officers Wilson and Jost are assigned to a patrol car and receive a call from the dispatcher to respond to a shooting at 236 Bever Street between Hoyt and Clinton Avenues. The two Officers arrive at the scene at 5:20 P.M. and see a man, later identified as David Smith of 242 Bever Street, lying on the sidewalk and bleeding from the chest. An ambulance arrives at 5:35 P.M., and the attendant, Peter Johnson, pronounces Mr. Smith dead from a gunshot wound on the left side of the chest. Officer Jost begins to walk along Bever Street looking for witnesses. Suddenly, William Jones comes out of his store, located at 239 Bever Street, and tells Officer Jost that he heard a gunshot at 5:15 P.M. and saw two White males going through the victim's pockets. Meanwhile, Walter Garvey, of 247 Bever Street, approaches Officer Wilson and tells him that he saw the victim fall to the ground and then observed two White males search the victim before they ran west on Bever Street toward Clinton Avenue. Mr. Garvey describes one suspect as having blonde hair and wearing a blue jacket with black jeans, and the other suspect as having brown hair and wearing a white jacket and blue jeans.

After interviewing Mr. Jones, Officer Jost is approached by Doris Finkle, owner of the Sweet Shop located at 238 Bever Street. She tells him that the victim was walking along Bever Street when two White males came from behind and pushed Mr. Smith against the wall. She also says that a man with blonde hair started talking to the victim when suddenly a man wearing a white jacket fired a gun and Mr. Smith fell to the ground. Mrs. Finkle tells the Officer that the two suspects searched the victim and then ran away.

15. Who pronounced David Smith dead?

    A. William Jones
    C. Peter Johnson
    B. Doris Finkle
    D. Walter Garvey

16. Which of the following persons was the FIRST to report hearing a gunshot?

    A. Police Officer Jost
    C. Peter Johnson
    B. Walter Garvey
    D. William Jones

17. Who was the FIRST witness to give a description of the suspects' clothing?

    A. Mrs. Finkle
    C. Mr. Jones
    B. Mr. Garvey
    D. Mr. Johnson

Questions 18-22.

DIRECTIONS: Questions 18 through 22 are to be answered SOLELY on the basis of the following passage.

At 10:30 P.M., while parked in front of a clothing store at 1925 First Avenue, Police Officers Cole and Reese received a radio call to investigate a possible burglary at 1423 Second Avenue. The Officers were to meet the complainant in front of the location given by the dispatcher.

Upon arriving at the scene, the Officers were met by Mr. Rivers, the owner of the Melody Grocery Store, located at 1425 Second Avenue. He explained that he had called the police because he noticed the bicycle shop next door had been left open. Mr. Rivers further stated that the shop owner, Mr. Rose, usually closes at 9:00 P.M. Mr. Reyes, who lives at 1923 First Avenue and works with Mr. Rivers, noticed that the store gate had been partially closed and upon checking saw that the lights were off and the door was not locked.

At 10:40 P.M., Police Officer Reese radioed for a Supervisor before entering the premises. Sgt. Parker arrived ten minutes later and supervised a search to find out if the owner was sick, injured, or incapacitated somewhere in the store. The results proved negative. Apparently nothing had been taken or disturbed, and there were no visible signs of forced entry. The Sergeant instructed Officer Reese to guard the premises while his partner contacted Police Officer Craig, the Precinct Telephone Switchboard Operator, who would check the precinct merchant index file and then notify Mr. Rose of the situation.

18. The Sergeant supervised a search to determine if the 18.____

    A. store was being burglarized
    B. owner was sick or injured
    C. store had been ransacked
    D. owner was working late

19. The police dispatcher received a call regarding a possible burglary at _____ Avenue. 19.____

    A. 1423 Second   B. 1923 First
    C. 1425 Second   D. 1925 First

20. What type of business was left unsecured? 20.____

    A. Florist shop   B. Bicycle shop
    C. Grocery store   D. Clothes store

21. At what time did the Sergeant arrive? _____ P.M. 21.____

    A. 10:30   B. 10:40   C. 10:45   D. 10:50

22. Which Police Officer would attempt to contact the store owner? 22.____

    A. Reese   B. Parker   C. Craig   D. Cole

Questions 23-25.

DIRECTIONS: Questions 23 through 25 are to be answered SOLELY on the basis of the following passage.

Housing Police Officer Lewis is patrolling Woodrow Houses, a housing project consisting of ten 14-story apartment buildings. Officer Lewis is working a Midnight to 8 A.M. tour of duty. Before going to his assigned post, Officer Lewis was told by Sergeant Smith that there has been an increase in the number of apartment burglaries on his post. Sergeant Smith also stated that the burglaries are occurring between 10 P.M. and 6 A.M. A male Hispanic, 5'5" tall, dark complexion, tattoo of a cross on right forearm, large black mustache, and wearing dark sunglasses has been seen in the area just prior to a number of the burglaries. At 3:00 A.M., Officer Lewis is patrolling his post and notices a male Hispanic, 5'5", dark complexion, no mustache, no sunglasses, a tattoo of a cross on his right forearm, exiting an apartment building carrying a portable TV and a Sony radio. Officer Lewis stops the man and asks him where he was coming from. The man says that he was just coming from his friend's 6th floor apartment and that he was going to have the TV and radio repaired in the morning. Officer Lewis asks the man to return to the apartment with him. The man then drops the TV and radio and starts to run. Officer Lewis pursues and apprehends the man and places him under arrest.

A short time later, Officer Lewis learns that a burglary had occurred in a 6th floor apartment in the same building that the male Hispanic was seen leaving. Among the items stolen were a TV and radio.

23. What did the male Hispanic have in his possession when he was stopped by Officer Lewis? A

    A. portable radio and a Sony TV
    B. portable TV and a Sony radio
    C. Sony TV and a Zenith radio
    D. Zenith TV and a Sony radio

24. Sergeant Smith informed Officer Lewis of burglaries occurring on his post

    A. late evening and early morning
    B. early morning and early afternoon
    C. early afternoon and late afternoon
    D. late morning and early evening

25. The man Officer Lewis stopped to question

    A. was about 5'5" tall and wore dark sunglasses
    B. had a dark complexion and a large black mustache
    C. had a large black mustache and a tattoo on his forearm
    D. had a tattoo on his forearm and was about 5'5" tall

KEY (CORRECT ANSWERS)

1.	B/C	11.	C
2.	A	12.	A
3.	A	13.	C
4.	D	14.	D
5.	B	15.	C
6.	C	16.	D
7.	D	17.	B
8.	B	18.	B
9.	B	19.	A
10.	D	20.	B

21. D
22. C
23. B
24. A
25. D

CODING

EXAMINATION SECTION

COMMENTARY

An ingenious question-type called coding, involving elements of alphabetizing, filing, name and number comparison, and evaluative judgment and application, has currently won wide acceptance in testing circles for measuring clerical aptitude and general ability, particularly on the senior (middle) grades (levels).

While the directions for this question usually vary in detail, the candidate is generally asked to consider groups of names, codes, and numbers, and then, according to a given plan, to arrange codes in alphabetic order; to arrange these in numerical sequence; to re-arrange columns of names and numbers in correct order; to espy errors in coding; to choose the correct coding arrangement in consonance with the given directions and examples, etc.

This question-type appear to have few parameters in respect to form, substance, or degree of difficulty.

Accordingly, acquaintance with, and practice in, the coding question is recommended for the serious candidate.

TEST 1

DIRECTIONS: Questions 1 through 8 are to be answered on the basis of the code table and the instructions given below.

Code Letter for Traffic Problem	B	H	Q	J	F	L	M	I
Code Number for Action Taken	1	2	3	4	5	6	7	8

Assume that each of the capital letters on the above chart is a radio code for a particular traffic problem and that the number immediately below each capital letter is the radio code for the correct action to be taken to deal with the problem. For instance, "1" is the action to be taken to deal with problem "B", "2" is the action to be taken to deal with problem "H", and so forth.

In each question, a series of code letters is given in Column 1. Column 2 gives four different arrangements of code numbers. You are to pick the answer (A, B, C, or D) in Column 2 that gives the code numbers that match the code letters in the same order.

SAMPLE QUESTION

Column 1
BHLFMQ

Column 2
A. 125678
B. 216573
C. 127653
D. 126573

According to the chart, the code numbers that correspond to these code letters are as follows: B – 1, M – 2, L – 6, F – 5, M – 7, Q – 3. Therefore, the right answer is 126573. This answer is D in Column 2.

2 (#1)

	Column 1	Column 2	
1.	BHQLMI	A. 123456 B. 123567 C. 123678 D. 125678	1._____
2.	HBJQLF	A. 214365 B. 213456 C. 213465 D. 214387	2._____
3.	QHMLFJ	A. 321654 B. 345678 C. 327645 D. 327654	3._____
4.	FLQJIM	A. 543287 B. 563487 C. 564378 D. 654378	4._____
5.	FBIHMJ	A. 518274 B. 152874 C. 528164 D. 517842	5._____
6.	MIHFQB	A. 872341 B. 782531 C. 782341 D. 783214	6._____
7.	JLFHQIM	A. 465237 B. 456387 C. 4652387 D. 4562387	7._____
8.	LBJQIFH	A. 614382 B. 6134852 C. 61437852 D. 61431852	8._____

KEY (CORRECT ANSWERS)

1. C
2. A
3. D
4. B
5. A
6. B
7. C
8. A

TEST 2

DIRECTIONS: Each question or incomplete statement is followed by several suggested answers or completions. Select the one that BEST answers the question or completes the statement. *PRINT THE LETTER OF THE CORRECT ANSWER IN THE SPACE AT THE RIGHT.*

Questions 1-5.

DIRECTIONS: Questions 1 through 5 are based on the following list showing the name and number of each of nine inmates.

1. Johnson   4. Thompson   7. Gordon
2. Smith   5. Frank   8. Porter
3. Edwards   6. Murray   9. Lopez

Each question consists of 3 sets of numbers and letters. Each set should consist of the numbers of three inmates and the first letter of each of their names. The letters should be in the same order as the numbers. In at least two of the three choices, there will be an error. On your answer sheet, mark only that choice in which the letters correspond with the numbers and are in the same order. If all three sets are wrong, mark choice D in your answer space.

SAMPLE QUESTION
A. 386 EPM
B. 542 FST
C. 474 LGT

Since 3 corresponds to E for Edwards, 8 corresponds to P for Porter, and 6 corresponds to M for Murray, choice A is correct and should be entered in your answer space. Choice B is wrong because letters T and S have been reversed. Choice C is wrong because the first number, which is 4, does NOT correspond with the first letter of choice C, which is L. It should have been T. If choice A were also wrong, then D would be the correct answer.

1. A. 382 EGS   B. 461 TMJ   C. 875 PLF   1._____
2. A. 549 FLT   B. 692 MJS   C. 758 GSP   2._____
3. A. 936 LEM   B. 253 FSE   C. 147 JTL   3._____
4. A. 569 PML   B. 716 GJP   C. 842 PTS   4._____
5. A. 356 FEM   B. 198 JPL   C. 637 MEG   5._____

Questions 6-10.

DIRECTIONS: Questions 6 through 10 are to be answered on the basis of the following information:

2 (#3)

In order to make sure stock is properly located, incoming units are stored as follows:

STOCK NUMBERS	BIN NUMBERS
00100 – 39999	D30, L44
40000 – 69999	14L, D38
70000 – 99999	41L, 80D
100000 and over	614, 83D

Using the above table, choose the answer A, B, C, or D, which lists the correct Bin Number for the Stock Number given.

6. 17243
   A. 41L   B. 83D   C. 14L   D. D30

7. 9219
   A. D38   B. L44   C. 614   D. 41L

8. 90125
   A. 41L   B. 614   C. D38   D. D30

9. 10001
   A. L44   B. D38   C. 80D   D. 83D

10. 200100
    A. 41L   B. 14L   C. 83D   D. D30

KEY (CORRECT ANSWERS)

1. B   6. D
2. D   7. B
3. A   8. A
4. C   9. A
5. C   10. C

TEST 3

DIRECTIONS: Each question or incomplete statement is followed by several suggested answers or completions. Select the one that BEST answers the question or completes the statement. *PRINT THE LETTER OF THE CORRECT ANSWER IN THE SPACE AT THE RIGHT.*

Questions 1-9.

DIRECTIONS: Assume that the Police Department is planning to conduct a statistical study of individuals who have been convicted of crimes during a certain year. For the purpose of this study, identification numbers are being assigned to individuals in the following manner:

The first two digits indicate the age of the individual.
The third digit indicates the sex of the individual:
    1. Male
    2. Female
The fourth digit indicates the type of crime involved:
    1. criminal homicide
    2. forcible rape
    3. robbery
    4. aggravated assault
    5. burglary
    6. larceny
    7. auto theft
    8. other
The fifth and sixth digits indicate the month in which the conviction occurred:
    01. January
    02. February, etc.

Questions 1 through 9 are to be answered SOLELY on the basis of the above information and the following list of individuals and identification numbers.

Name	Number	Name	Number
Abbott, Richard	271304	Morris, Chris	212705
Collins, Terry	352111	Owens, William	231412
Elders, Edward	191207	Parker, Leonard	291807
George, Linda	182809	Robinson, Charles	311102
Hill, Leslie	251702	Sands, Jean	202610
Jones, Jackie	301106	Smith, Michael	42108
Lewis, Edith	402406	Turner, Donald	191601
Mack, Helen	332509	White, Barbara	242803

1. The number of women on the above list is
   A. 6   B. 7   C. 8   D. 9

2. The two convictions which occurred during February were for the crimes of
   A. aggravated assault and auto theft
   B. auto theft and criminal homicide
   C. burglary and larceny
   D. forcible rape and robbery

   2._____

3. The ONLY man convicted of auto theft was
   A. Richard Abbott   B. Leslie Hill
   C. Chris Morris   D. Leonard Parker

   3._____

4. The number of people on the list who were 25 years old or older is
   A. 6   B. 7   C. 8   D. 9

   4._____

5. The OLDEST person on the list is
   A. Terry Collins   B. Edith Lewis
   C. Helen Mack   D. Michael Smith

   5._____

6. The two people on the list who are the same age are
   A. Richard Abbott and Michael Smith
   B. Edward Elders and Donald Turner
   C. Linda George and Helen Mack
   D. Leslie Hill and Charles Robinson

   6._____

7. A 28-year-old man who was convicted of aggravated assault in October would have identification number
   A. 281410   B. 281509   C. 282311   D. 282409

   7._____

8. A 33-year-old woman convicted in April of criminal homicide would have identification number
   A. 331140   B. 331204   C. 332014   D. 332104

   8._____

9. The number of people on the above list who were convicted during the first six months of the year is
   A. 6   B. 7   C. 8   D. 9

   9._____

Questions 10-19.

DIRECTIONS: The following is a list of patients who were referred by various clinics to the laboratory for tests. After each name is a patient identification number. Questions 10 through 19 are to be answered on the basis of the information contained in this list and the explanation accompanying it.

The first digit refers to the clinic which made the referral:
1. cardiac   6. Hematology
2. Renal   7. Gynecology
3. Pediatrics   8. Neurology
4. Ophthalmology   9. Gastroenterology
5. Orthopedics

3 (#2)

The second digit refers to the sex of the patient:
1. male
2. female

The third and fourth digits give the age of the patient

The last two digits give the day of the month the laboratory tests were performed

LABORATORY REFERRALS DURING JANUARY

Adams, Jacqueline	320917	Miller, Michael	511806
Black, Leslie	813406	Pratt, William	214411
Cook, Marie	511616	Rogers, Ellen	722428
Fisher, Pat	914625	Saunders, Sally	310229
Jackson, Lee	923212	Wilson, Jan	416715
James, Linda	624621	Wyatt, Mark	321326
Lane, Arthur	115702		

10. According to the list, the number of women referred to the laboratory during January was
    A. 4   B. 5   C. 6   D. 7

11. The clinic from which the MOST patients were referred was
    A. Cardiac
    B. Gynecology
    C. Ophthalmology
    D. Pediatrics

12. The YOUNGEST patient referred from any clinic other than Pediatrics was
    A. Leslie Black
    B. Marie Cook
    C. Arthur Lane
    D. Sally Saunders

13. The number of patients whose laboratory tests were performed on or before January 16 was
    A. 7   B. 8   C. 9   D. 10

14. The number of patients referred for laboratory tests who are under age 45 is
    A. 7   B. 8   C. 9   D. 10

15. The OLDEST patient referred to the clinic during January was
    A. Jacqueline Adams
    B. Linda James
    C. Arthur Lane
    D. Jan Wilson

16. The ONLY patient treated in the Orthopedics clinic was
    A. Marie Cook
    B. Pat Fisher
    C. Ellen Rogers
    D. Jan Wilson

17. A woman, age 37 was referred from the Hematology clinic to the laboratory. Her laboratory tests were performed on January 9.
    Her identification number would be
    A. 610937   B. 623709   C. 613790   D. 623790

18. A man was referred for lab tests from the Orthopedics clinic. He is 30 years old and his tests were performed on January 6.
    His identification number would be
    A. 413006   B. 510360   C. 513006   D. 513060

    18.____

19. A 4-year-old boy was referred from the Pediatrics clinic to have laboratory tests on January 23.
    His identification number was
    A. 310422   B. 310423   C. 310433   D. 320403

    19.____

KEY (CORRECT ANSWERS)

1. B	11. D
2. B	12. B
3. B	13. A
4. D	14. C
5. D	15. D
6. B	16. A
7. A	17. B
8. D	18. C
9. C	19. B
10. B	

TEST 4

DIRECTIONS: Each question or incomplete statement is followed by several suggested answers or completions. Select the one that BEST answers the question or completes the statement. *PRINT THE LETTER OF THE CORRECT ANSWER IN THE SPACE AT THE RIGHT.*

Questions 1-10.

DIRECTIONS: Questions 1 through 10 are to be answered on the basis of the information and directions given below.

Assume that you are a Senior Stenographer assigned to the personnel bureau of a city agency. Your supervisor has asked you to classify the employees in your agency into the following five groups:

- A. Employees who are college graduates, who are at least 35 years of age but less than 50, and who have been employed by the City for five years or more;
- B. Employees who have been employed by the City for less than five years, who are not college graduates, and who earn at least $32,500 a year but less than $34,500;
- C. Employees who have been City employees for five years or more, who are at least 21 years of age but less than 35, and who are not college graduates;
- D. Employee who earn at least $34,500 a year but less than $36,000 who are college graduates, and who have been employed by the City for less than five years;
- E. Employees who are not included in any of the foregoing groups.

NOTE: In classifying these employees you are to compute age and period of service as of <u>January 1, 2003</u>. In all cases, it is to be assumed that each employee has been employed continuously in City service. <u>In each question, consider only the information which will assist you in classifying each employee Any information which is of no assistance in classifying an employee would not be considered.</u>

SAMPLE: Mr. Brown, a 29-year-old veteran, was appointed to his present position of Clerk on June 1, 2000. He has completed two years of college. His present salary is $33,050.

The correct answer to this sample is B, since the employee has been employed by the City for less than five years, is not a college graduate, and earn at least $32,500 a year but less than $34,500.

Questions 1 through 10 contain excerpts from the personnel records of 10 employees in the agency. In the correspondingly numbered space at the right print the capital letter preceding the appropriate group into which you would place each employee.

1. Mr. James has been employed by the City since 1993, when he was graduated from a local college. Now 35 years of age, he earns $36,000 a year.   1.____

2. Mr. Worth began working in City service early in 1999. He was awarded his college degree in 1994, at the age of 21. As a result of a recent promotion, he now earns $34,500 a year.   2.____

2 (#4)

3. Miss Thomas has been a City employee since August 1, 1998. Her salary is $34,500 a year. Miss Thomas, who is 25 years old, has had only three years of high school training.

3.____

4. Mr. Williams has had three promotions since entering City service on January 1, 1991. He was graduated from college with honors in 1974, when he was 20 years of age. His present salary is $37,000 a year.

4.____

5. Miss Jones left college after two years of study to take an appointment to a position in the City service paying $33,300 a year. She began work on March 1, 1997 when she was 19 years of age.

5.____

6. Mr. Smith was graduated from an engineering college with honors in January 1998 and became a City employee three months later. His present salary is $35,810. Mr. Smith was born in 1976.

6.____

7. Miss Earnest was born on May 31, 1979. Her education consisted of four years of high school and one year of business school. She was appointed as a typist in a City agency on June 1, 1997. Her annual salary is $33,500.

7.____

8. Mr. Adams, a 24-year-old clerk, began his City service on July 1, 1999, soon after being discharged from the U.S. Army. A college graduate, his present annual salary is $33,200.

8.____

9. Miss Charles attends college in the evenings, hoping to obtain her degree is 2004, when she will be 30 years of age. She has been a City employee since April 1998, and earns $33,350.

9.____

10. Mr. Dolan was just promoted to his present position after six years of City service. He was graduated from high school in 1982, when he was 18 years of age, but did not go on to college. Mr. Dolan's present salary is $33,500.

10.____

KEY (CORRECT ANSWERS)

1.	A	6.	D
2.	D	7.	C
3.	E	8.	E
4.	A	9.	B
5.	C	10.	E

TEST 5

DIRECTIONS: Questions 1 through 4 each contain five numbers that should be arranged in numerical order. The number with the lowest numerical value should be first and the number with the highest numerical value should be last. Pick that option which indicates the CORRECT order of the numbers.

Examples: A. 9; 18; 14; 15; 27
B. 9; 14; 15; 18; 27
C. 14; 15; 18; 27; 9
D. 9; 14; 15; 27; 18

The correct answer is B, which contains the proper arrangement of the five numbers.

1. A. 20573; 20753; 20738; 20837; 20098
   B. 20098; 20753; 20573; 20738; 20837
   C. 20098; 20573; 20753; 20837; 20738
   D. 20098; 20573; 20738; 20753; 20837

2. A. 113492; 113429; 111314; 113114; 131413
   B. 111314; 113114; 113429; 113492; 131413
   C. 111314; 113429; 113492; 113114; 131413
   D. 111314; 113114; 131413; 113429; 113492

3. A. 1029763; 1030421; 1035681; 1036928; 1067391
   B. 1030421; 1029763; 1035681; 1067391; 1036928
   C. 1030421; 1035681; 1036928; 1067391; 1029763
   D. 1029763; 1039421; 1035681; 1067391; 1036928

4. A. 1112315; 1112326; 1112337; 1112349; 1112306
   B. 1112306; 1112315; 1112337; 1112326; 1112349
   C. 1112306; 1112315; 1112326; 1112337; 1112349
   D. 1112306; 1112326; 1112315; 1112337; 1112349

KEY (CORRECT ANSWERS)

1. D
2. B
3. A
4. C

TEST 6

DIRECTIONS: The phonetic filing system is a method of filing names in which the alphabet is reduced to key code letters. The six key letters and their equivalents are as follows:

KEY LETTERS	EQUIVALENTS
b	p, f, v
c	s, k, g, j, q, x, z
d	t
l	none
m	n
r	none

A key letter represents itself.
Vowels (a, e, i, o, and u) and the letters w, h, and y are omitted.
For example, the name GILMAN would be represented as follows:
    G is represented by the key letter C.
    I is a vowel and is omitted.
    L is a letter and represents itself.
    M is a key letter and represents itself.
    A is a vowel and is omitted.
    N is represented by the key letter M.

Therefore, the phonetic filing code for the name GILMAN is CLMM.

Answer Questions 1 through 10 based on the information below.

1. The phonetic filing code for the name FITZGERALD would be
    A. BDCCRLD   B. BDCRLD   C. BDZCRLD   D. BTZCRLD

2. The phonetic filing code CLBR may represent any one of the following names EXCEPT
    A. Calprey   B. Flower   C. Glover   D. Silver

3. The phonetic filing code LDM may represent any one of the following names EXCEPT
    A. Halden   B. Hilton   C. Walton   D. Wilson

4. The phonetic filing code for the name RODRIGUEZ would be
    A. RDRC   B. RDRCC   C. RDRCZ   D. RTRCC

5. The phonetic filing code for the name MAXWELL would be
    A. MCLL   B. MCWL   C. MCWLL   D. MXLL

6. The phonetic filing code for the name ANDERSON would be
    A. AMDRCM   B. ENDRSM   C. MDRCM   D. NDERCN

7. The phonetic filing code for the name SAVITSKY would be
    A. CBDCC   B. CBDCY   C. SBDCC   D. SVDCC

8. The phonetic filing code CMC may represent any one of the following names EXCEPT 8._____
   A. James B. Jayes C. Johns D. Jones

9. The ONLY one of the following names that could be represented by the phonetic filing code CDDDM would be 9._____
   A. Catalano B. Chesterton C. Cittadino D. Cuttlerman

10. The ONLY one of the following names that could be represented by the phonetic filing code LLMCM would be 10._____
    A. Ellington B. Hallerman C. Inslerman D. Willingham

KEY (CORRECT ANSWERS)

1.	A	6.	C
2.	B	7.	A
3.	D	8.	B
4.	B	9.	C
5.	A	10.	D

NAME AND NUMBER CHECKING
EXAMINATION SECTION
TEST 1

DIRECTIONS: This test is designed to measure your speed/and accuracy. You are urged to work both quickly and accurately and to do correctly as many lists as you can in the time allowed. The test consists of lists or pairs of names and numbers. Count the number of IDENTICAL pairs in each list. Then, select the correct number, 1, 2, 3, 4, 5, and indicate your choice in the space at the right. Two sample questions are presented for your guidance, together with the correct solutions.

SAMPLE LIST A
Adelphi College	– Adelphia College
Braxton Corp	– Braxeton Corp.
Wassaic State School	– Wassaic State School
Central Islip State Hospital	– Central Isllip State Hospital
Greenwich House	– Greenwich House

NOTE: There are only two correct pairs—Wassaic State School and Greenwich House. Therefore, the CORRECT answer is 2.

SAMPLE LIST B
78453694	– 78453684
784530	– 784530
533	– 534
67845	– 67845
2368745	– 2368755

NOTE: There are only two correct pairs—784530 and 67845. Therefore, the CORRECT answer is 2.

LIST 1   1.____
    98654327   - 98654327
    74932564   - 7492564
    61438652   - 61438652
    01297653   - 01287653
    1865439765   - 1865439765

LIST 2   2.____
    478362   - 478363
    278354792   - 278354772
    9327   - 9327
    297384625   - 27384625
    6428156   - 6428158

2 (#1)

LIST 3   3.____
    Abbey House   - Abbey House
    Actor's Fund Home   - Actor's Fund Home
    Adrian Memorial   - Adrian Memorial
    A. Clayton Powell Home   - Clayton Powell House
    Abbot E. Kittredge Club   - Abbott E. Kitteredge Club

LIST 4   4.____
    3682   - 3692
    21937453829   - 31927453829
    723   - 733
    2763920   - 2763920
    47293   - 47293

LIST 5   5.____
    Adra House   - Adra House
    Adolescents' Court   - Adolescents' Court
    Cliff Villa   - Cliff Villa
    Clark Neighborhood House   - Clark Neighborhood House
    Alma Mathews House   - Alma Mathews House

LIST 6   6.____
    28734291   - 28734271
    63810263849   - 63810263846
    26831027   - 26831027
    368291   - 368291
    7238102637   - 7238102637

LIST 7   7.____
    Albion State T.S.   - Albion State T.C.
    Clara de Hirsch Home   - Clara De Hirsch Home
    Alice Carrington Royce   - Alice Carington Royce
    Alice Chopin Nursery   - Alice Chapin Nursery
    Lighthouse Eye Clinic   - Lighthouse Eye Clinic

LIST 8   8.____
    327   - 329
    712438291026   - 712438291026
    2753829142   - 275382942
    826287   - 826289
    26435162839   - 26435162839

LIST 9   9.____
    Letchworth Village   - Letchworth Village
    A.A.A.E. Inc.   - A.A.A.E. Inc.
    Clear Pool Camp   - Clear Pool Camp
    A.M.M.L.A. Inc.   - A.M.M.L.A. Inc.
    J.G. Harbard   - J.G. Harbord

3 (#1)

LIST 10   10.____
    8254   - 8256
    2641526   - 2641526
    4126389012   - 4126389102
    725   - 725
    76253917287   - 76253917287

LIST 11   11.____
    Attica State Prison   - Attica State Prison
    Nellie Murrah   - Nellie Murrah
    Club Marshall   - Club Marshal
    Assissium Casea-Maria   - Assissium Casa-Maria
    The Homestead   - The Homestead

LIST 12   12.____
    2691   - 2691
    623819253627   - 623819253629
    28637   - 28937
    278392736   - 278392736
    52739   - 52739

LIST 13   13.____
    A.I.C.P. Boys Camp   - A.I.C.P. Boy's Camp
    Einar Chrystie   - Einar Christyie
    Astoria Center   - Astoria Center
    G. Frederick Brown   - G. Federick Browne
    Vacation Service   - Vacation Services

LIST 14   14.____
    728352689   - 728352688
    643728   - 643728
    37829176   - 37827196
    8425367   - 8425369
    65382018   - 65382018

LIST 15   15.____
    E.S. Streim   - E.S. Strim
    Charles E. Higgins   - Charles E. Higgins
    Baluvelt, N.Y.   - Blauwelt, N.Y.
    Roberta Magdalen   - Roberto Magdalen
    Ballard School   - Ballard School

LIST 16   16.____
    7382   - 7392
    281374538299   - 291374538299
    623   - 633
    6273730   - 6273730
    63392   - 63392

LIST 17
- Orrin Otis — - Orrin Otis
- Barat Settlement — - Barat Settlemen
- Emmanuel House — - Emmanuel House
- William T. McCreery — - William T. McCreery
- Seamen's Home — - Seaman's Home

17.____

LIST 18
- 72824391 — - 72834371
- 3729106237 — - 37291106237
- 82620163849 — - 82620163846
- 37638921 — - 37638921
- 82631027 — - 82631027

18.____

LIST 19
- Commonwealth Fund — - Commonwealth Fund
- Anne Johnsen — - Anne Johnson
- Bide-A-Wee Home — - Bide-a-Wee Home
- Riverdale-on-Hudson — - Riverdal-on-Hudson
- Bialystoker Home — - Bailystoker Home

19.____

LIST 20
- 9271 — - 9271
- 392918352627 — - 392018852629
- 72637 — - 72637
- 927392736 — - 927392736
- 92739 — - 92739

20.____

LIST 21
- Charles M. Stump — - Charles M. Stump
- Bourne Workshop — - Buorne Workshop
- B'nai Bi'rith — - B'nai Brith
- Poppenhuesen Institute — - Poppenhuesen Institute
- Consular Service — - Consular Service

21.____

LIST 22
- 927352689 — - 927352688
- 647382 — - 648382
- 93729176 — - 93727196
- 649536718 — - 649536718
- 5835367 — - 5835369

22.____

LIST 23
- L.S. Bestend — - L.S. Bestent
- Hirsch Mfg. Co. — - Hircsh Mfg. Co.
- F.H. Storrs — - F.P. Storrs
- Camp Wassaic — - Camp Wassaic
- George Ballingham — - George Ballingham

23.____

5 (#1)

LIST 24 24.____
    372846392048   - 372846392048
    334   - 334
    7283524678   - 7283524678
    7283   - 7283
    7283629372   - 7283629372

LIST 25 25.____
    Dr. Stiles Company   - Dr. Stills Company
    Frances Hunsdon   - Frances Hunsdon
    Northrop Barrert   - Nothrup Barrent
    J.D. Brunjes   - J.D. Brunjes
    Theo. Claudel & Co.   - Theo. Claudel co.

KEY (CORRECT ANSWERS)

1.	3	11.	3
2.	1	12.	3
3.	2	13.	1
4.	2	14.	2
5.	5	15.	2
6.	3	16.	2
7.	1	17.	3
8.	2	18.	2
9.	4	19.	2
10.	3	20.	4

21.	2
22.	1
23.	2
24.	5
25.	2

TEST 2

DIRECTIONS: This test is designed to measure your speed/and accuracy. You are urged to work both quickly and accurately and to do correctly as many lists as you can in the time allowed. The test consists of lists or pairs of names and numbers. Count the number of IDENTICAL pairs in each list. Then, select the correct number, 1, 2, 3, 4, 5, and indicate your choice in the space at the right.

LIST 1
    82728   - 82738
    82736292637   - 82736292639
    728   - 738
    83926192527   - 83726192529
    82736272   - 82736272

1.____

LIST 2
    L. Pietri   - L. Pietri
    Mathewson, L.F.   - Mathewson, L.F.
    Funk & Wagnall   - Funk & Wagnalls
    Shimizu, Sojio   - Shimizu, Sojio
    Filing Equipment Bureau - Filing Equipment Buraeu

2.____

LIST 3
    63801829374   - 63801839474
    283577657   - 283577657
    65689   - 65689
    3457892026   - 3547893026
    2779   - 2778

3.____

LIST 4
    August Caille   - August Caille
    The Well-Fare Service   - The Wel-Fare Service
    K.L.M. Process co.   - R.L.M. Process Co.
    Merrill Littell   - Merrill Littell
    Dodd & Sons   - Dodd & Son

4.____

LIST 5
    998745732   - 998745733
    723   - 723
    463849102983   - 463849102983
    8570   - 8570
    279012   - 279012

5.____

LIST 6
    M.A. Wender   - M.A. Winder
    Minneapolis Supply Co. - Minneapolis Supply Co.
    Beverly Hills Corp   - Beverley Hills Corp.
    Trafalgar Square   - Trafalgar Square
    Phifer, D.T.   - Phiefer, D.T.

6.____

2 (#2)

LIST 7 7._____
    7834629   - 7834629
    3549806746   - 3549806746
    97802564   - 97892564
    689246   - 688246
    2578024683   - 2578024683

LIST 8 8._____
    Scadrons'   - Scadrons'
    Gensen & Bro.   - Genson & Bro.
    Firestone Co.   - Firestone Co.
    H.L. Eklund   - H.L. Eklund
    Oleomargarine Co.   - Oleomargarine Co.

LIST 9 9._____
    782039485618   - 782039485618
    53829172639   - 63829172639
    892   - 892
    82937482   - 829374820
    52937456   - 53937456

LIST 10 10._____
    First Nat'l Bank   - First Nat'l Bank
    Sedgwick Machine Works   - Sedgewick Machine Works
    Hectographia Co.   - Hectographia Corp.
    Levet Bros.   - Levet Bros.
    Multistamp Co., Inc.   - Multistamp Co., Inc.

LIST 11 11._____
    7293   - 7293
    6382910293   - 6382910292
    981928374012   - 981928374912
    58293   - 58393
    18203649271   - 283019283745

LIST 12 12._____
    Lowrey Lb'r Co.   - Lowrey Lb'r Co.
    Fidelity Service   - Fidelity Service
    Reumann, J.A.   - Reumann, J.A.
    Duophoto Ltd.   - Duophotos Ltd.
    John Jarratt   - John Jaratt

LIST 13 13._____
    6820384   - 6820384
    383019283745   - 383019283745
    63927102   - 63928102
    91029354829   - 91029354829
    58291728   - 58291728

LIST 14
    Standard Press Co.   - Standard Press Co.
    Reliant Mf'g. Co.   - Relant Mf'g Co.
    M.C. Lynn   - M.C. Lynn
    J. Fredericks Company   - G. Fredericks Company
    Wandermann, B.S.   - Wanderman, B.S.

14.____

LIST 15
    4283910293   - 4283010203
    992018273648   - 992018273848
    620   - 629
    752937273   - 752937373
    5392   - 5392

15.____

LIST 16
    Waldorf Hotel   - Waldorf Hotel
    Aaron Machinery Co.   - Aaron Machinery Co.
    Caroline Ann Locke   - Caroline Ane Locke
    McCabe Mfg. Co.   - McCabe Mfg. Co.
    R.L. Landres   - R.L. Landers

16.____

LIST 17
    68391028364   - 68391028394
    68293   - 68293
    739201   - 739201
    72839201   - 72839211
    739917   - 739719

17.____

LIST 18
    Balsam M.M.   - Balsamm, M.M.
    Steinway & Co.   - Stienway & M. Co.
    Eugene Elliott   - Eugene A. Elliott
    Leonard Loan Co.   - Leonard Loan Co.
    Frederick Morgan   - Frederick Morgen

18.____

LIST 19
    8929   - 9820
    392836472829   - 392836572829
    462   - 4622039271
    827   - 2039276837
    53829   - 54829

19.____

LIST 20
    Danielson's Hofbrau   - Danielson's Hafbrau
    Edward A. Truarme   - Edward A. Truame
    Insulite Co.   - Insulite Co.
    Reisler Shoe Corp.   - Rielser Shoe Corp.
    L.L. Thompson   - L.L. Thompson

20.____

4 (#2)

LIST 21
    92839102837   - 92839102837
    58891028   - 58891028
    7291728   - 7291928
    272839102839   - 272839102839
    428192   - 428102

21.____

LIST 22
    K.L. Veiller   - K.L. Veiller
    Webster, Roy   - Webster, Ray
    Drasner Spring Co.   - Drasner Spring Co.
    Edward J. Cravenport   - Edward J. Cravanport
    Harold Field   - Harold A. Field

22.____

LIST 23
    2293   - 2293
    4283910293   - 5382910292
    871928374012   - 871928374912
    68293   - 68393
    8120364927   - 81293649271

23.____

LIST 24
    Tappe, Inc   - Tappe, Inc.
    A.M. Wentingworth   - A.M. Wentinworth
    Scott A. Elliott   - Scott A. Elliott
    Echeverria Corp.   - Echeverria Corp.
    Bradford Victor Company   - Bradford Victer Company

24.____

LIST 25
    4820384   - 4820384
    393019283745   - 283919283745
    63917102   - 63927102
    91029354829   - 91029354829
    48291728   - 48291728

25.____

KEY (CORRECT ANSWERS)

1.	1	11.	1
2.	3	12.	3
3.	2	13.	4
4.	2	14.	2
5.	4	15.	1
6.	2	16.	3
7.	3	17.	2
8.	4	18.	1
9.	2	19.	1
10.	3	20.	2

21. 3
22. 2
23. 1
24. 2
25. 4

www.ingramcontent.com/pod-product-compliance
Lightning Source LLC
Chambersburg PA
CBHW082213300426
44117CB00016B/2783